VICTORIA REVEALED

500 facts about the Queen and her world

*Deirdre Murphy and Lee Prosser,
Margaret Dorman, Sebastian Edwards, Sarah Kilby,
Alexandra Kim, Clare Murphy,
Louise Nash, David Souden and Lucy Worsley*

CONTENTS

INTRODUCTION

Queen Victoria in 1887, the 50th year of her reign.

What does the Victorian age mean to us now, more than a century after its end? It is a fitting testimony that after so long the image of Queen Victoria, staring disdainfully into the distance, swathed in lace and with the little diamond crown perched on her head, remains instantly recognisable. Her statues grace towns all over the world and the physical remains of that time surround us everywhere we go. We continue to live in her world. Despite a hundred years of rapacious development, the Victorian buildings which fill our towns are familiar reminders of what some people consider to be a golden age. As a personality, Queen Victoria has become semi-divine with the passage of time. This was a process that began even before she died in 1901, when many people were acutely aware that they were 'Victorians' and that her death represented the end of an era.

In more recent times, some people have viewed the 19th century as a golden age when Britannia ruled the waves, when hard work bred success and firm rules of etiquette meant people had excellent manners. The term 'Victorian values' has entered modern parlance. It is an over-simplistic idea that has been hijacked by politicians but still it conveys a powerful aspiration for a supposedly idyllic past. The view of the Victorian age as a golden period when unfettered progress, rising standards of living and Britain's enormous economic power made life easier has been cultivated assiduously by elderly relatives with fading, second-hand memories. But the word 'Victorian' can also be used as a term of abuse. It also means old-fashioned, repressed, grimy, oppressive, and so the age is one that is very complicated.

But what of reality? It would be too simple to treat the 19th century as if it were one homogenous period. Our image of the Victorian era is coloured somewhat by films, television programmes which project a two-dimensional picture. The Victorian age, like Queen Victoria herself, was multi-faceted. The period was marked by immense technological, cultural and economic change that continues to define our own age, our national identity and those of the many nations around the world from the former British Empire. At the same time, an obsession with death and sentimentality, cluttered, claustrophobic interiors, Jack the Ripper, music halls, industrial pollution, poverty, disease and urban squalor are just a few things which might spring to mind if given only a minute to assess the period.

In 1819, the year Queen Victoria was born, when her grandfather King George III was on the throne, the country was essentially rural. It was shaped in part by the industrial revolution but a coach and horses was the only way to get around. The pace of life was slow, the economy was fairly undeveloped and large areas of the world were still unexplored. But the Victorians were supremely self-confident and they understood the possibilities of their technology. They embraced innovation and inventiveness. Even at Victoria's accession in 1837 the signs of change were everywhere, and the young Queen came to the throne in a spirit of optimism and a break with the past.

By the time of her death in 1901, the country had been transformed out of all recognition. The population had doubled and the burgeoning cities were transformed into sprawling metropolitan centres with hordes of commuters making the daily trudge to their office jobs. Trains sped around the country and coal-fired, steam-driven ships criss-crossed the globe. Iron had replaced timber

in buildings, gas had given way to electricity and communicating by telephone was now possible. Intense economic growth had created an insatiable appetite for raw materials and new markets – dots on the map had become enormous nations-in-the-making. But some of these advancements came at a price. Densely populated cities produced filthy, crowded slums where people lived in abject poverty. The Great Famine of 1846 had exposed deep-rooted social and political problems in Ireland; many 'little wars' emerged as Britain sought to assert itself in the world.

Society had also changed. Mass production had transformed Britain into a nation of consumers, with money to spare and leisure time, thanks to the new public holidays. They had libraries and public parks in which to better themselves and improved civil and voting rights. Traditional hierarchical society was giving way to more democratic ideals. Ideas of social welfare and human rights became more widespread and philosophers such as John Stuart Mill advocated equality of the sexes. These ideals were of course not yet achieved, but they were notions that were put in place during the Victorian period.

What of the Queen herself, as a personality, divorced from the world to which she has become so closely identified? Now, she is perhaps most closely associated with her romance with Prince Albert, the frosty 'we are not amused' epithet, her many children, becoming the grandmother of Europe and, of course, her black widow's clothes. Again, the story is complex. On the one hand, she was dowdy, a stuffy personality, recording the minutiae of a dreary life in the journals that she demanded her daughter Princess Beatrice censor after her death. Victoria constantly interfered in politics, making her personal prejudices against ministers and other politicians known. Yet she was also a lively, witty and funny woman who was no snob. She was often surprisingly clear of prejudice and learned the Hindustani language from one of her Indian servants. She loved the theatre, was an accomplished artist and musician and she adored Gilbert and Sullivan.

Victoria kept a journal from the age of 13 until the end of her life. These surviving accounts offer detailed reports of her daily activities and together with the letters she wrote to her relatives, friends and ministers provide deeply personal insights into the key events that dominated her life. During her lonely, isolated childhood at Kensington Palace she depended on the few people she learned she could trust. Her accession in 1837 marked a break from her mother's tight hold on her. The 18-year-old Queen was inexperienced but her self-confidence won the respect of her ministers. She fell head over heels in love with Prince Albert, who she married in 1840. She remained absolutely devoted to him, remarking how lucky she was to have her 'angel' by her side. Prince Albert's death in 1861 tore her life apart. It led to a long, despondent and almost self-indulgent period of grief from which she would, or could, not emerge.

Queen Victoria was the first global personality. She was not a powerful ruler but instead presided as a figurehead over a rapidly-evolving machine of state, culture and empire. Innovations in printing and, later, photography and moving film enabled the distribution of her image on an international scale. Reports of her public activities appeared regularly in newspapers across the British Empire. The public appetite for details of her private life remained steady throughout her reign. The excerpts from her own journals, *Leaves from the Journal of our Life in the Highlands*, which she published in 1868, sold out in three months. Her Diamond Jubilee, which marked her 60 years on the throne, was celebrated around the world. On the day of the celebrations, she thanked her subjects for their loyalty with a telegraph message that was sent across the Empire.

The Victorians are still with us in many respects. We live and work in their buildings, we play in their parks, we are entertained in their theatres and educated in their museums and libraries. When we catch a train to the seaside, paddle in the sea, eat fish and chips, and send a postcard home we are still following closely in the footsteps of our Victorian ancestors, albeit in more relaxed attire!

Some distinctly modern aspects of our lives today have their roots in the Victorian period. The internet, or the idea of instant communication on a global scale, would not have been possible without the telegraph machine. We have pioneers such as Eadweard Muybridge and Robert W Paul who captured moving images of Queen Victoria's Diamond Jubilee celebrations in 1897 to thank for the films we watch. Education for all, social equality and the universal right to vote developed from Victorian ideas.

When the Queen died as the 20th century dawned, her image had solidified into that of a semi-glorified figure. She was a pillar of respectability, the mother of a nation. Her continued presence during such an intense period of technological, economic and social change had helped to place the monarchy at the core of the nation's identity. She had drawn much of the British Empire into a firm, almost personal relationship with her. For Europe's royal families, the relationship was in fact personal – she was their matriarch, and numbered kings and queens among her descendants.

Thanks in part to the mass media, Victoria's image has endured, even if it is not viewed entirely uncritically. Today, she remains a compelling symbol of strength and uncompromising morality, a bastion of old-fashioned formality who was surprisingly modern.

Deirdre Murphy and Lee Prosser

VICTORIA AS A GIRL

The sudden death in childbirth of Princess Charlotte, only daughter of George IV, prompted a desperate race among his brothers to produce an heir. Their attempts left the tiny Princess Victoria next in line. She had been born and brought up at Kensington Palace by her widowed mother, the Duchess of Kent. Through the 'Kensington System', the Duchess and her aide, Sir John Conroy, isolated the young Princess, cutting her off from the outside world and enforcing a strict education programme designed to prepare her for her future role. Victoria had few friends of her own age, and doted on her beloved pet spaniel Dash and her pony, Rosy. Despite her mother's best attempts to control her every move, the secluded and lonely Princess Victoria's iron will rang through. On her first day as queen, after years under her mother's watch, the 18-year-old Victoria demanded to be alone.

BIRTH AND CHILDHOOD

Victoria spent her childhood living at Kensington Palace which, despite former glory, had become a rather run-down, ramshackle retirement home for minor royals. Even as a little girl, it was possible to glimpse in her the stubborn and independent traits of a future queen.

1

Although Victoria's parents, the Duke and Duchess of Kent were royal, they were not wealthy. They were glad to have been given rooms in Kensington Palace. Victoria was born on 24 May 1819 in what is now the North Drawing Room. She was a healthy baby, described by her grandmother, the Dowager Duchess of Saxe-Coburg, as 'plump as a partridge'.

2

She was christened on 24 June 1819 in the Cupola Room. There was a great row about what her name was to be! It was only decided at the last possible moment because her uncle, King George IV, peevishly rejected the various alternatives Victoria's parents had proposed, including Elizabeth and Charlotte. The names finally chosen were 'Alexandrina Victoria'.

3

Victoria later wrote that her earliest memory was of crawling upon a yellow carpet at Kensington Palace. She also took her first steps at the palace. A pair of her tiny black baby shoes *(above)* survive.

4

By the age of five, Victoria was already endearing herself to those around her.

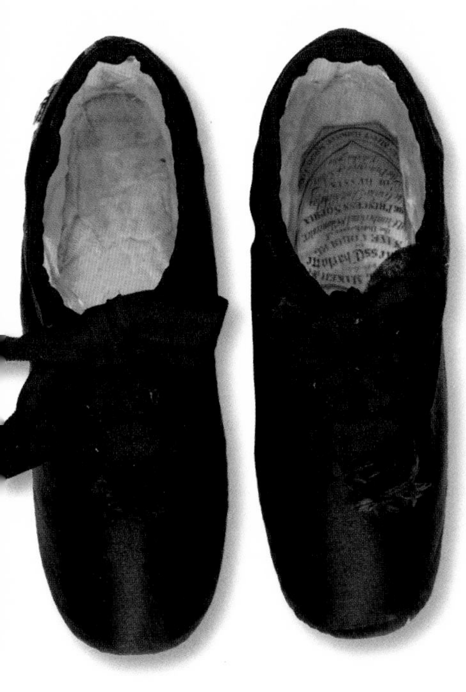

Previous page: Victoria as an extremely cute 7-year-old. This lovely enamel portrait by William Essex reproduces a painting of the young Princess that the Queen commissioned in *c*1841 as a Christmas present for Albert.

This page **Left to right:** Princess Victoria by Johann Georg Paul Fischer, 1819; Informal sketch by of the Princess by Lady Elizabeth Keith Heathcote, a friend of Victoria's mother, during a holiday in Ramsgate *c*1822; Victoria's baby shoes; Princess Victoria aged 4, by Stephen Poyntz Denning, 1823.

Her grandmother described the little girl's morning routine:
'In the morning, she sometimes does not want to get out of bed, preferring to tell all sorts of tales. Lehzen [her governess] takes her gently from her bed, and sits her down on the thick carpet, where she has to put on her stockings. One has to contain oneself not to burst out laughing, when she says in a tragic tone of voice, "Poor Vicky! She is an unhappy child! She just doesn't know which is the right stocking and which is the left! I am an unhappy child!"'

5

Lord Albemarle, a frequent visitor to Kensington Palace, remembered how he used 'to watch from the window the movements of a bright pretty little girl, seven years of age. It was amusing to see how impartially she divided the contents of the watering pot between the flowers and her own little feet'.

6

When she was 10, Victoria's governess showed her the royal family tree, and the princess realised that she could eventually become queen herself. 'I see I am nearer to the throne than I thought', she is reported to have said, adding, after a pensive moment, 'I will be good'.

7

The young princess's behaviour was recorded in what was called her 'Good Behaviour Book', which was read by her over-controlling mother and strict governess. Despite her good intentions, Victoria frequently railed against their restrictions. On 24 September 1832, she wrote that she'd been 'VERY VERY VERY VERY HORRIBLY NAUGHTY!!!!'

8

Victoria's first encounter with 'ordinary' people's lives came as a shock. She made her first tour of Wales as a very sheltered 13-year-old. 'The country is very desolate', she wrote of the first industrial area she saw: 'engines flaming, coals, in abundance, everywhere, smoking and burning coal heaps, intermingled with wretched huts and carts and little ragged children'.

9

As a wilful teenager, Victoria disliked doing her piano practice. 'You must practise like everyone else', her teacher told her. But the princess simply slammed the lid down. 'There! There is no must about it.'

10

In the autumn of 1835, 16-year-old Victoria fell desperately ill with typhoid. While she was weak and sick, the Duchess of Kent's aide, the manipulative Sir John Conroy tried to get her to sign over her power to him. But Victoria refused, giving an early glimpse of the iron that lay within her soul.

YOUNG VICTORIA AS ARTIST AND SUBJECT

As a young princess, Victoria was given drawing lessons by Richard Westall. She greatly enjoyed sketching her favourite actors and dancers from the theatre as well as people in her household. She kept drawing for the rest of her life.

11

Mother and daughter *(left)* In this portrait, a copy by Henry Bone after William Beechey *c*1824, the young Princess holds a miniature of her dead father, the Duke of Kent. The Duchess was a very dominant figure in Victoria's early life and controlled every aspect of her upbringing. Even before this painting was made it was known that it was very likely that Victoria would inherit the throne.

12

The princess and the pony *(above)* Victoria loved to ride and often mentioned her pony Rosy in her journals. This is an early sketch, *c*1820s, by the Princess, before she had drawing lessons.

13

By royal appointment *(right)* A contemplative 10-year-old Victoria is captured in this drawing of 1829 by Richard James Lane, who was later appointed royal lithographer by the Queen in 1837. Lane later executed several portraits in pencil or chalk of the Queen, and most of the royal family at various ages.

14

Victoria sketching *(right, top)* Drawing master Richard Westall captures Victoria in 1830 in a rather fanciful setting. Westall was an English painter and a prolific illustrator of both fiction and poetry, but perhaps best known for his portraits of Lord Byron. He taught Victoria for eight years, and she found him to be an excellent, patient teacher. Victoria was talented and her love of drawing was passed to some of her children.

15

Royal variety *(right, bottom)* While on an early 'royal progress' around the country in 1832, Victoria and her mother visited Chatsworth House. Victoria was enthralled by seeing charades for the first time. Afterwards, she described the game in detail in her journal and drew this sketch of Sir Walter Scott's story *Kenilworth* being performed.

16

Lehzen and Dash *(next page)* Victoria used coloured chalks to sketch two of her closest friends: Baroness Lehzen, her governess, and her pet King Charles spaniel Dash, *c*1833. 'Dearest Lehzen'

as Victoria often referred to her in her diaries, was the Princess's only adult confidante during her cloistered girlhood, and she took her beloved governess with her to Buckingham Palace after she became queen.

17

Queen in the making *(right)* This lovely portrait of the young Princess (and Dash), painted by Sir George Hayter was given to Victoria's uncle Leopold, King of the Belgians in 1836. Leopold arranged for his nephew Prince Albert to visit Victoria in the well-founded hopes that a match would be made. Victoria fell madly in love with her handsome cousin and they were married in 1840. A shared passion for art helped their happy marriage; the couple often sketched and painted together. Victoria chose Hayter as her 'Portrait and Historical Painter' and in 1841 he was appointed 'Principal Painter in Ordinary' to the Queen.

18

Dash in trousers *(below)* This anonymous drawing of Dash being painted by his owner *c*1833 must have delighted the Princess. Victoria adored the patient-tempered little dog, whom she bathed regularly and often dressed up for fun! (See also Fact 43)

19

At the ballet *(right)* Marie Taglioni was Victoria's favourite ballet dancer and she saw her dance many times. Here she draws the dancer in *La Sylphide*, 1834. Victoria copied this costume for one of many wooden dolls that she and her governess, Baroness Lehzen, dressed.

20

Self-portrait *(bottom right)* Victoria sketched this charming image *c*1832 after her drawing lessons started to take effect. Victoria was always reluctant to sacrifice accuracy for the sake of artistry, so we know that her drawings were as realistic as she could make them.

TEN QUEEN MAKERS AND SHAKERS

The young Victoria was tugged every which way between various relatives and advisers, in particular her mother and her mother's 'adviser' (possibly also her lover) – the ambitious Sir John Conroy. They sought to control Victoria through a regime which became known as the 'Kensington System'.

21

The Duchess of Kent Later in life, Victoria claimed that she had not been 'on a comfortable or at all intimate or confidential footing with my mother'. However, Victoria's earliest surviving letter reads: 'My dear Mamma I love you. Victoria', and despite the rows of her teenage years, they grew closer when she became a mother herself.

22

Sir John Conroy Sir John *(above)* had been a trusted aide to Victoria's late father, and maintained a mesmerising hold over his widow. The other courtiers speculated about their relationship. One of them said to the Duke of Wellington that he suspected that Conroy was the Duchess's lover. The Duke is alleged to have replied that he 'supposed so'.

23

George IV Victoria's uncle, the ageing George IV was overweight, rarely seen in public and addicted to laudanum. However, while the lively young Princess Victoria made a good impression upon her 'Uncle King', she didn't see much of him, and so escaped being associated with his unpopular image.

24

William IV When George IV died in 1830, his younger brother William became king. This bluff, hearty, simple-minded man, very different from his brother, was well-disposed towards Victoria personally although he viewed her mother as a pushy ogre who sought to use her daughter for her own ends. None of William's legitimate children survived, so his niece Victoria became his heir.

Left to right: An imposing portrait of the scheming Sir John Conroy (detail) painted by Henry William Pickersgill; Louise, Baroness Lehzen, by Carl Friedrich Koepke, c1842; Princess Feodora by John Haslem, 1847; Luigi Lablache, by Franz Xaver Winterhalter, 1852.

25

Princess Feodora *(above)* Victoria's childhood was not completely friendless: for at least part of it, she was accompanied by her beloved elder half-sister, Feodora. Jealous of Feodora's influence, Sir John Conroy campaigned successfully to have her married off and sent to live in Germany. 'How I love you, dearest sister', wrote Feodora to Victoria sadly, once the Channel lay between them, 'and how often I think of you and long to see you'.

26

Baroness Lehzen Lehzen, *(left)* born in Hanover, was Victoria's governess, close supporter and the sworn enemy of Sir John Conroy. Lehzen did not shine academically, but she gave Victoria a firm set of values. One could 'pardon wickedness in a Queen', Lehzen insisted, 'but not weakness'. (See also Fact 49)

27

Leopold, King of the Belgians Leopold, who was Victoria's favourite uncle, was a member of the Coburg family, and became a British prince when he married Victoria's cousin Charlotte in 1816. After Charlotte's early death, Leopold kept a watchful eye on Victoria. He introduced her to his nephew Albert, with sensational results.

28

Baroness Späth Until she was sacked by Victoria's mother, Späth, another governess, had been on Victoria's 'side' and supported her in the tense atmosphere at Kensington.

29

Luigi Lablache, her much-admired singing teacher Victoria's singing teacher, Luigi Lablache *(right)* was one of the few people in Victoria's childhood to represent fun and freedom. Of Irish and French extraction, he had a terrific bass voice, and was noted for his comic performances. Victoria loved to see him sing at the opera, and it was her own idea to have him as her singing tutor. (See also Fact 48.) In his 'lessons' he and Victoria would simply sing together. Lablache had married singer Teresa Pinotti in 1813 with whom he had 13 children, several of them good singers.

30

Edward, Duke of Kent Victoria's late father, who died when she was a baby, was notable by his absence in her life. The fourth son of George III, Edward was an unsuccessful and tyrannical army officer. He was shunted off to Gibraltar, where it was felt that he could not do too much damage, and lived there with his long-term mistress, Madame de Saint-Laurent. When George IV's daughter Charlotte died unexpectedly in 1817, the Duke of Kent had to leave the faithful Madame de Saint-Laurent and marry a German princess with the hope of ensuring the royal line. This he did by fathering Victoria in 1819, but he died the very next year , leaving Victoria and her mother, the Duchess, little but debt.

'DEAR DIARY...'

Victoria's diary, which she began in 1832 and kept for the rest of her life, faithfully recorded her activities and impressions of the people she met. When she was young, her journal was read by her mother and governess so we can assume it was an honest (although probably self-censored) account.

I was VERY much amused

31

It was clear to see what Victoria enjoyed as a girl. She was a keen horsewoman and rode whenever she could.

Saturday 13 April 1833 'At 12 we went out riding in the park with Victoire, Lehzen and Sir John. It was a *delightful* ride. We cantered a good deal. SWEET LITTLE ROSY went BEAUTIFULLY!!'

32

Victoria marked her early birthdays with enthusiasm:

Friday 24 May 1833 'I am to-day fourteen years old! How *very old*!!'

She politely listed a copious amount of presents in painstaking detail, but the highlight of the day was a Juvenile Ball, given at St James's Palace in her honour, which she described with her now famous line 'I was *very much* amused.'

33

For the sheltered young princess, trips out of the world of Kensington and into society must have held much excitement and a break from boredom. A trip to the opera provided her with a talking point.

Saturday 19 April 1834 'We came in just at the beginning of the Opera of *Anna Boulena*. The characters were: Anna Boulena, Mdlle. Guiletta Grisi. She is a most beautiful singer and actress and is likewise very young and pretty...M Perrot (whom I had never seen before) danced likewise quite beautifully. We went away as soon as the 2nd act of the opera was over. We came home at 12. I was VERY MUCH AMUSED INDEED!'

34

From her mid-teens, a new sense of maturity begins to creep into her diary. On her birthday she reflects:

Sunday 24 May 1835 'Today is my 16th birthday! How very old that sounds; but I feel that the two years to come till I attain my 18th are the most important of any almost. I now only begin to appreciate my lessons, and hope from this time on, to make great progress.'

35

Pets, some exotic, were an important diversion in Victoria's childhood.

Tuesday 25 August 1835 'At 4 we walked out [in Kensington Gardens] with Lady Flora and Lehzen and came home at 5 minutes to 5. In our walk we met a man with beautiful parrots. Amongst them was one dear little paroquet of a green colour with a pale brown head and so very tame that Mamma took it on her finger and it would hardly leave her. It talks also, the man says. It is not so remarkable for its fine plumage than for its great tameness. Mamma bought the dear little thing. It is now in Mamma's room.'

What a happiness was it for me to throw myself into the arms of that *dearest* of Uncles

Walter Scott is my *beau idéal* of a poet

36

Occasionally, Victoria ventured further afield than London, which she greatly enjoyed after the solitude of Kensington. While staying in Bishopthorpe with the Archbishop of York she wrote:

Saturday 5 September 1835 'After dinner Lady Norreys and her cousin Miss Vernon sang a duet from *La Gazza Ladra* beautifully, and also "Suoni la tromba". They are both extremely pretty. They are pupils of Tamburini. We sang something then. I like Miss Vernon's voice the best of the two. We then went to prayers. After that I sang the Barcarola from *Faliero*, frightened to death. I stayed up till a 1/4 to 11'.

37

Victoria's Uncle Leopold had been married to her cousin Charlotte, and was a very important influence on the young princess.

Thursday 29 September 1835
'At length Uncle appeared, having Aunt Louisa at his arm. What a happiness was it for me to throw myself in the arms of that *dearest* of Uncles, who has always been to me like a father, and whom I love so *very dearly*! I had not seen him for 4 years and 2 months!'

38

Baroness Lehzen appears often in this book, a testament to her importance. In the Princess's own words after a serious illness:

Thursday 5 November 1835 *Dear good* Lehzen takes such care of me, and is so unceasing in her attentions to me, that I shall never be able to repay her sufficiently for it but by my love and gratitude. I never can sufficiently repay her for all she has *borne* and done for me. She is the *most affectionate, devoted, attached,* and *disinterested* friend I have, and I love her most *dearly*.'

39

Victoria's appreciation of art and literature was born in her early years, and included occasional visits from luminaries of the day. Some she hero-worshipped:

Tuesday 1 November 1836 'Oh! Walter Scott is my *beau idéal* of a Poet; I do so admire him both in Poetry and Prose!'

40

This was Victoria's day of destiny, when she was woken to be told that she had become queen. Life would never be the same again and the young sovereign confided her thoughts to her diary.

Tuesday 20 June 1837 'Since it has pleased Providence to place me in this station, I shall do my utmost to fulfil my duty towards my country; I am very young and perhaps in many, though not in all things, inexperienced, but I am sure, that very few have more real good will and more real desire to do what is fit and right than I have.'

I am very young and perhaps in many, though not in all things, inexperienced

TEN GIRLHOOD FAVOURITES

Victoria led a very isolated childhood at Kensington Palace. Her only playmates were her half-sister Feodora, who left England in 1828, and Victoire, daughter of Sir John Conroy. Nevertheless, the Princess took delight in animals and her love of the theatre, both interests which she maintained for many years.

41

Her dolls Princess Victoria delighted in her veritable palace-full of 132 tiny wooden dolls, which she named after society ladies and her idols from the theatre. The intricate clothes that she and Baroness Lehzen made for them were probably inspired by the dresses worn by fashionable visitors to Kensington Palace.

42

Sir Walter Scott His novel *The Bride of Lammermoor* was one of the few the young Victoria was permitted to read. Scott only met the Princess once, when her mother, the Duchess of Kent, invited him to dine with them at Kensington Palace in 1828. He later remarked that her confined upbringing was not the best training for a future queen.

43

Dash, her dog The 13-year-old Victoria quickly adopted Dash, the King Charles spaniel that Sir John Conroy gave to her mother in 1833. Dash offered some light relief to her secluded life at Kensington Palace. On 23 April 1833, she wrote, 'I dressed dear sweet little Dash for the second time after dinner in a scarlet jacket and blue trousers'. Immediately after her coronation in 1838, Victoria gave Dash a bath.

44

Horses The Princess rode frequently in Kensington Gardens, and occasionally further afield, which offered her moments of relative freedom. She also enjoyed trips in her pony phaeton. Victoria passed on her love of horses to her own children, who all had riding lessons.

45

Music Perhaps as an escape from her very solitary life, Princess Victoria loved to sing and play the piano. According to her journals, her day was punctuated with time spent at the piano, and she would ask many of her visitors to gather round and sing together.

46

The ballet Victoria's early journals contain enthusiastic descriptions of her frequent visits to the theatre, opera and ballet. In June 1833, when the Princess

Left to right: Princess Victoria in her pony phaeton by James Doyle, 1829; Some survivors of Victoria's collection of 132 dolls, fashionably dressed by the Princess and her governess; Victoria's pets, *Hector, Nero and Dash, with the parrot, Lory* painted by Sir Edwin Landseer in 1838.

watched the celebrated ballerina Marie Taglioni in *La Sylphide* she was thrilled. She drew illustrations of Taglioni's performance in her sketchbook and dressed one of her dolls as the ballerina.

47

A gypsy family Victoria became fascinated by the gypsy camp near Claremont House, Uncle Leopold's residence in Surrey. She visited the gypsies several times during her stay in 1836, and became deeply concerned with their welfare. With the help of her mother and Lehzen, Victoria sent them fuel and food, as well as a little knitted jacket for one woman's newborn baby.

48

Luigi Lablache On her 16th birthday, the Italian bass baritone Luigi Lablache joined a line-up of Victoria's favourite singers in a concert at Kensington Palace. He became her tutor a year later. Victoria enjoyed these lessons immensely. In August 1836 as his stay in London ended she wrote, 'I shall count the weeks and months eagerly till next April when I shall resume my delightful lessons with him.'

49

Her governess Baroness Lehzen's devotion to the Princess, supporting her against her mother and the manipulative John Conroy was hugely valued by Victoria, who kept her former governess close even after she became queen.

50

Drawing and painting The artist Richard Westall gave the princess her first drawing lesson in 1827. These weekly lessons formed a more pleasurable part of the Princess's rigid education schedule, the 'Kensington System'.

VICTORIA THE WOMAN

It is very tempting to regard Queen Victoria as a dour and sombre woman, a reputation which has been enhanced by the erroneously attributed expression, 'we are not amused'. In fact, Victoria was a complex personality, full of contradictions. At times, she could be authoritative and utterly fearsome. At others, she was deeply sentimental and over-dependent on her husband Prince Albert.

Her private secretary, Sir Henry Ponsonby, remarked on the uniqueness of her character, noting her unconventional nature and unorthodox views. The Queen's journals and letters reveal a stubborn, loving, self-confident, neurotic, impulsive woman who once even called herself 'too passionate' as she felt things so intensely. She was said to have had an infectious laugh, 'full of girlish glee'.

PHYSICAL VICTORIA

Victoria was very short, and as everyone knows, rather stout by the end of her life, when she looked almost spherical. However, nature also gave Victoria many gifts, including a 'very good' bust.

51

As a baby Victoria was described as a 'pretty little Princess'. Yet she would never be a beauty. She had blue eyes, 'large and full', and slightly frog-like like her grandfather George III's. 'A more homely little thing you never beheld', wrote one person who met her.

52

She was strong of character *and* strong of body! As a child she was called more of a 'pocket Hercules, than a pocket Venus'. As she later admitted, she was 'very much indulged by everyone and set pretty well all at defiance'. 'She is incredibly precocious for her age and very comical', commented her grandmother, 'I have never seen a more alert and forthcoming child.'

53

Victoria was vaccinated against smallpox in 1819, 1827 and 1835. This was a relatively new medical treatment and she seems to have survived it without ill effects.

54

Victoria preferred portraits where the painter had kindly depicted her with her lips shut. One of her associates wrote that 'her mouth, which is her worst feature, is generally a little open; her teeth small and short, and she shows her gums when she laughs, which is rather disfiguring'. (Yet the laugh itself was 'particularly delightful', full of 'girlish glee'.)

55

In later life she had bad teeth, yet hated treatment. 'I fear H.M. expects impossibilities from the dentists', wrote one, while another complained that she was 'very troublesome about her artificial teeth'.

56

Victoria lived as a child with her German mother and governess, so her first tutor had to work hard to eliminate her slight German accent. The British would want a queen who sounded like them when she spoke!

57

The young Victoria was described as a 'little princess [who] eats a little too much, and almost always a little too fast'. She suffered from serious obesity later in life; in 1867 she was described as 'growing enormously fat'. At Kensington Palace there is a pair of under garments of the mature Queen's *(below)*. They are embroidered with her monogram on the ample waist band, which measures 135cm (53ins)!

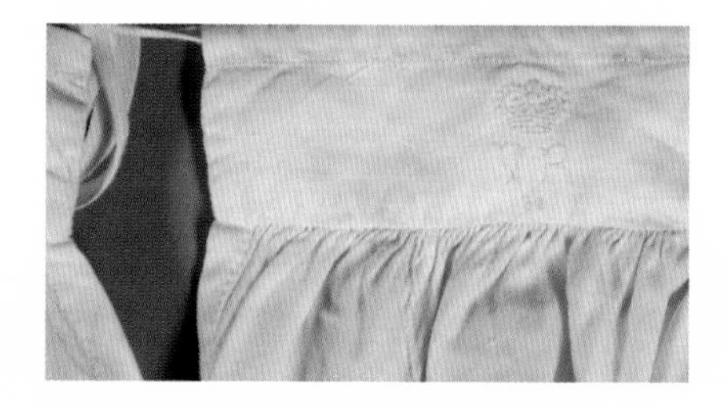

58

Victoria was very short, and later in life she lost a couple of inches from her already inconsiderable height. A tape-measure survives which records her height in 1838 as being 1.53m (5ft 1in). However, 'her bust', wrote another person who knew her, 'like most English women's is very good'.

Previous page: Queen Victoria by Franz Xaver Winterhalter, 1847 (detail). The Queen gave this portrait to Prince Albert on their seventh wedding anniversary.

This page **Left to right:** Victoria as a hefty infant, painted by Johann Georg Paul Fischer in 1819; A rare shot of the Queen smiling, snapped in 1887 by Charles Knight; The mature Queen's under garments; Victoria's excellent posture (and tiny feet in dancing slippers) are revealed in this portrait of 1832 by Alexandre-Jean Dubois Drahonet; Victoria as a tiny toddler, c1822. She is actually five months older than her taller playmate. Drawing by Lady Elizabeth Keith Heathcote.

59

Victoria had excellent posture. She was described as moving 'with grace, ease and lightness'. This was partly the result of strict deportment exercises when she was little. She did, though, have a problem in descending the stairs: Thomas Sully, her American portrait painter, noted that 'this does not proceed from any defect in the foot or ankle, but I fear from something wrong in the knee'.

60

The Queen was an accomplished dancer; in her youth she was very light on her delicate little feet! One of Victoria's shoes, traced on 10 October 1834, was 21.3cm (8.4in) long, which corresponds to a tiny modern British size 2!

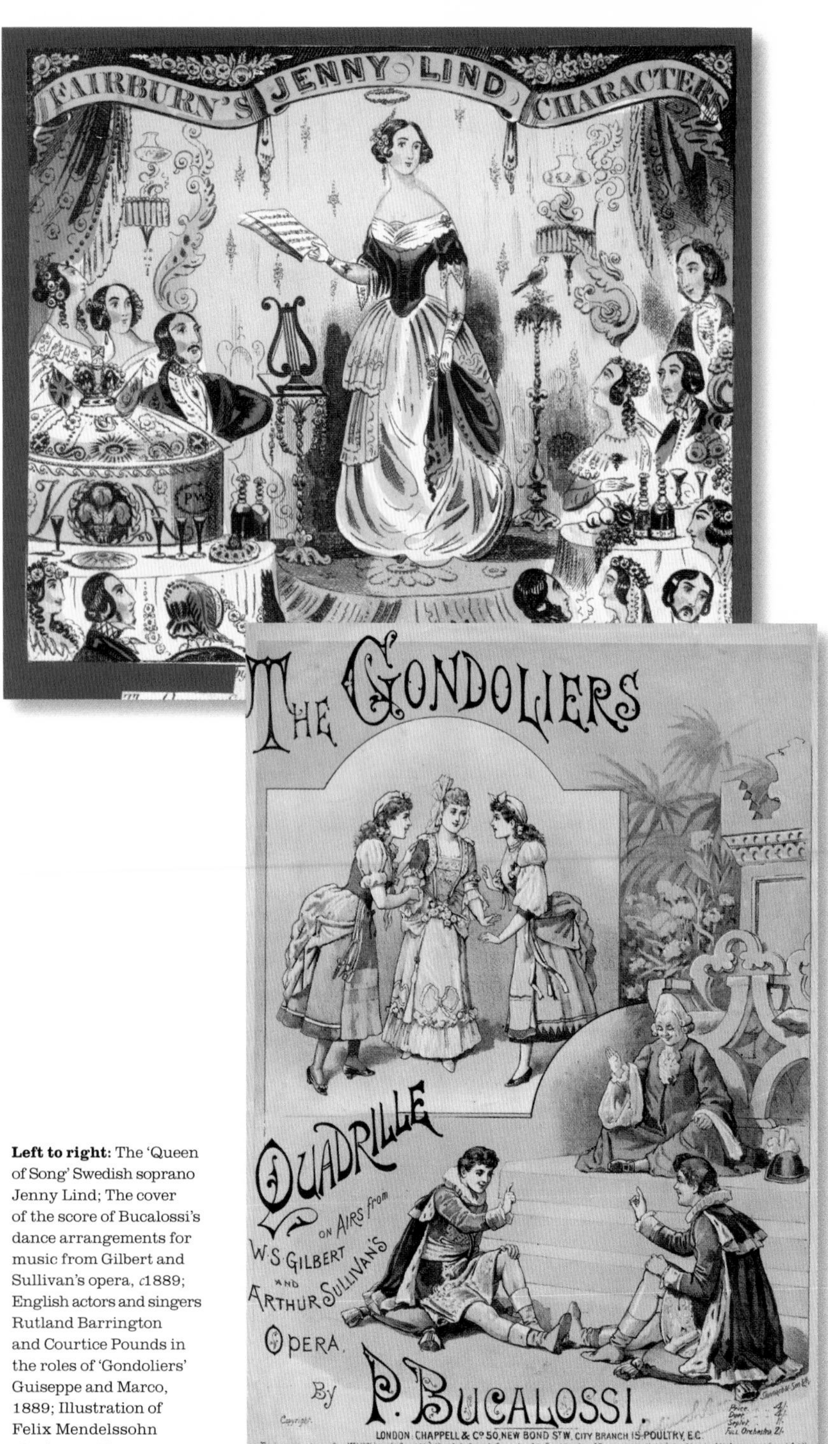

Left to right: The 'Queen of Song' Swedish soprano Jenny Lind; The cover of the score of Bucalossi's dance arrangements for music from Gilbert and Sullivan's opera, *c*1889; English actors and singers Rutland Barrington and Courtice Pounds in the roles of 'Gondoliers' Guiseppe and Marco, 1889; Illustration of Felix Mendelssohn playing to Victoria and Albert.

61

Untitled song written and composed in commemoration of Victoria's visit to Chatsworth in October 1832. The seclusion of Princess Victoria's early years was broken when her mother, the Duchess of Kent, decided to introduce her to the public through a series of visits around England and Wales. A music book owned by the Duchess of Kent contains this song from their enjoyable time at Chatsworth, when fellow guests played charades and performed scenes from *Tom Thumb.*

62

Rossini's opera *The Barber of Seville.* As a princess, Victoria loved her frequent excursions to the theatre with her mother, the Duchess of Kent. On 13 April 1833 she recorded, 'we were very much disappointed for Taglioni did not make her début, nor Rubini. We had only one scene of Il Barbiere di Siviglia, in which Signor Tambourini, who is a beautiful singer and actor, appeared, and Donizelli'.

63

Handel's *Messiah.* This was not a hit with the 16-year-old Princess. After hearing the Messiah during a visit to York in September 1835, Victoria wrote, 'I must say that with the exception of a few Choruses and one or two songs, it is very heavy and tiresome…I am not at all fond of Handel's music, I like the present Italian school such as Rossini, Bellini, Donizetti.'

VICTORIA'S TOP TEN

Music was an incredibly important part of Victoria's life from a young age, and central to her relationship with Prince Albert, who composed several pieces for her. She reviewed many of the performance she attended in her journals, demonstrating strong opinions and a deep understanding of music and opera.

64

Dem Fernen (To the Distant One), by Prince Albert. The day after Queen Victoria proposed to Prince Albert in October 1839, she recorded in her journal that he sang one of his own compositions to her and she then sang to him. The couple exchanged many letters and gifts before their wedding on 10 February the following year.

65

Bellini's *I Puritani*. Princess Victoria watched several performances of this opera during her early years, the most notable of which included the Italian singer Giulia Grisi, who the Princess greatly admired. Later, it was the first opera that Victoria and Prince Albert attended together and it therefore held a special place in her memory.

66

Song without words F Mendelssohn, 1847. The German composer arranged several pieces for Queen Victoria and Prince Albert to play together. Between 1842 and 1847, he paid several informal visits to the royal couple and he sent this song to Prince Albert on 7 May 1847, during his last visit to London.

67

Robert le Diable by Giacomo Meyerbeer, performed by Jenny Lind, 1847. Queen Victoria and Prince Albert were particularly enthralled with the 'Swedish Nightingale' Jenny Lind. They attended all 16 of the singer's performances during her London debut season at Her Majesty's Theatre in 1847. (See also Fact 242)

68

Mascagni's *Cavelleria Rusticana*. From an early age, Victoria preferred the high drama and romance of Italian operas over Handel's 'tiresome' oratorios. On 26 November 1891 she described Mascagni's *Cavelleria Rusticana* in her journal, 'The story was most pathetic and touching beyond words.'

69

The Gondoliers William S Gilbert and Sir Authur Sullivan, 1889. While Victoria's interests lay principally with Italian opera, she was fond of the more popular operettas by Gilbert and Sullivan including *The Gondoliers*, which was performed at Windsor Castle in 1891. The Queen once asked Sir Arthur Sullivan in casual conversation when he was going to write a proper opera. He took her comment seriously and after various struggles with his creative partner Gilbert, he produced *Ivanhoe*, which was a huge hit at the Royal English Opera House (now the Palace Theatre, London).

70

Wagner's *Lohengrin*. On her 80th birthday, the Queen listened to a performance of *Lohengrin* in the Waterloo Gallery at Windsor. She wrote in her journal, 'I was simply enchanted. It is the most glorious composition, so poetic, so dramatic, and one might almost say, religious in feeling and full of sadness, pathos, and tenderness.'

VICTORIA'S STYLE

While fashion was not one of Victoria's great interests – she wrote very little about clothes in her daily journal entries – her surviving garments mark some of the most important events in her life.

71

Great Exhibition dress, 1851 The Queen wore a dress of pink silk *(above)* woven with interlocking silver circles to the Crystal Palace for the opening of the grandly-titled Great Exhibition of the Works of Industry of All Nations on 1 May 1851. She was immensely proud of Prince Albert's central role in organising the magnificent festival.

72

Mourning dress, 1862 After Prince Albert's sudden death in 1861, Queen Victoria was determined that he should not be forgotten. The black-clad court served as a visual reminder of the nation's loss. While the restrictions at court eventually relaxed, the Queen remained in mourning for the rest of her life. The dress is at the Museum of London and is the earliest of her surviving mourning clothes.

73

Military jacket, 1850s As Commander-in-Chief of the army, Queen Victoria held several reviews of the troops as they returned home from the Crimean War in 1856. She wore a military-inspired red wool jacket, decorated with gold braid and buttons. Prince Albert may have designed the jacket for her, as there was no military uniform for women.

74

Dressing gown, 1840-50 A gown of extremely fine, white cotton is the earliest surviving example of the Queen's personal linen. The delicate gathers and precise stitching are typical of Victoria's night wear and undergarments, which were all of the highest quality.

75

Parliamentary robes, 1838-51 Queen Victoria's crimson silk velvet mantle and kirtle *(right)* were probably woven in London's Spitalfields area. They were then made up by a robemaker, complete with gold lace and ermine trim.

76

Evening dress, about 1843 The young Queen's wardrobe was filled with brightly-coloured dresses in light fabrics. Sadly, only a handful of dresses survive from that period, often given as gifts after use. The Queen gave one as a souvenir to the wife of John Gregory Crace, whom Prince Albert had introduced to the

Queen. John Crace helped to design the Medieval Court in the Great Exhibition of 1851.

77

Wedding dress, 1840 Before her wedding to Prince Albert on 10 February, Queen Victoria researched 18th-century royal precedents such as the attire worn at the wedding of George III in 1761. To ensure she did not outshine Albert, she decided against wearing the customary red velvet robe of state as other monarchs had done. Instead, she wore a simple cream silk satin gown *(right)* with court train, which is now often credited with starting a vogue for the white wedding dress.

Previous page **Far left:** Victoria in pink silk at the opening of the Great Exhibition, 1851, by Henry Courtney Selous. **Left:** the Queen in parliamentary robes, painted by Franz Xaver Winterhalter, 1859. **Centre:** Painting of the wedding by Sir George Hayter, 1840-2. **Right:** Victoria's wedding dress.

This page **Far left:** Brocaded silk dress designed in 1851 by Eugène Lami for a costume ball. **Left:** a dress worn by the teenaged Victoria, woven to imitate the fashionable tartan, **Below:** *The First Council of Queen Victoria*, by Sir David Wilkie, 1838.

78

Fancy dress, 1851 Eugène Lami designed this ivory and gold moiré and brocaded silk dress *(far left)* for the Stuart ball which was held at Buckingham Palace on 13 June 1851. This 'modern' interpretation of 17th-century fashion was one of several fancy dress costumes that the Queen commissioned. For the Bal Costumé in 1842, she and Prince Albert had dressed as Queen Philippa and King Edward III. Victoria 'permitted' the publication of a souvenir album of the designs after the event. It was hoped that promotion of the 2,000 or so costumes would create work for Spitalfields silk weavers, many of whom were unemployed.

79

Velvet dress, 1835-7 A silk velvet dress *(left)* that Princess Victoria wore as a teenager is woven with coloured horizontal and vertical stripes to imitate tartan. A pair of later tartan shawls also survive in the Royal Ceremonial Dress Collection. These checked fabrics were both fashionable and reflected the Queen's love for all things Scottish.

80

Privy Council dress, 1837 The 18-year-old Victoria wore this dress (which was originally black, but has discoloured over time) on the morning of 20 June 1837 for her first Privy Council meeting in the Red Saloon at Kensington Palace. The young Queen was in mourning for her uncle, William IV, who had died in the middle of the night. However, for his painting of the event, shown above, Sir David Wilkie asked Victoria to wear a white dress to emphasise her youth and vulnerability, and so she would stand out against all the black-clad councillors.

VICTORIA'S JEWELS

The crowns, insignia and other state jewellery that Victoria wore formed an important element of her queenly image. The Queen also treasured her intensely personal jewellery: gifts from Prince Albert, family and friends and commemorative pieces she commissioned herself.

81

The Oriental Circlet *(above)* Around 1853, Prince Albert directed the production by R S Garrard & Co of this spectacular eastern-inspired gold, diamond and ruby tiara, which was originally set with more than 2,600 diamonds. Albert was inspired by the Indian jewels presented to the Queen at the conclusion of the Great Exhibition in 1851, and the design features 'Mughal' arches framing lotus flowers. The Prince took great interest in Victoria's jewellery. His Christmas and birthday presents to her often included pieces he designed himself. 'Albert has such taste & always arranges everything for me about my jewels,' wrote Victoria.

82

Brooch by Magdalena Dalton *(above right)* This copy of a miniature of Prince Albert by Sir William Ross was Queen Victoria's favourite image of her husband and was made by Rundell, Bridge and Rundell. The Queen wore it constantly – hence its faded condition. Several portrait artists depicted her wearing it.

83

Gold locket Princess Victoria's mother, gave her a gold locket (not shown), containing a lock each of her parents' hair, on 24 May 1820, her first birthday. Victoria's father, Edward, Duke of Kent, had died only four months earlier.

84

Wedding brooch *(far right)* Prince Albert gave this simple brooch, composed of an enormous oval sapphire surrounded by diamonds, to Victoria on the day before their wedding in February 1840. She wore it on their wedding day and continued to wear it regularly until Albert's death in 1861.

85

The Koh-i-Nûr diamond This enormous stone originated in central southern India and, making its convoluted way via the Mughal treasury and the Persian warrior Nadir Shah, was received by Queen Victoria from the East India

Company in 1850. Thinking it not brilliant enough, she had the 186-carat diamond re-cut with more facets. Victoria wore it as a brooch *(see portrait, left)* and in a circlet; on her death it became part of the Crown Jewels and is now in the crown of Queen Elizabeth, The Queen Mother, made in 1937.

86

Orange blossom parure *(Over page)*
Pretty and delicate, this suite of gold, porcelain and enamel orange blossom jewellery includes a brooch which was one of the first gifts Prince Albert sent to Victoria during their engagement in 1839. In an accompanying letter, he wrote, 'may you think with love of your faithful Albert

when you take it into your hand'. Victoria wore parts of the parure on every wedding anniversary while Albert was alive.

87

Sapphire and diamond tiara
(shown in portrait right) In 1842, Victoria was painted by Franz Xaver Winterhalter wearing this diamond and sapphire tiara, which was probably designed by Prince Albert. Victoria wears the tiara in an unconventional style: low on the back of her head, arranged over her fashionable plaited and looped hairstyle. The tiara is complemented by the diamond and sapphire brooch which Albert gave Victoria for their wedding.

88

Queen Victoria's small diamond crown *(above)* The grieving Queen withdrew from public life after Prince Albert's death in 1861. However, following mounting criticism she made a muted return to public life. This tiny crown, only 9.4cm (3.7in) high, designed for her in 1870 and set with over 1,000 diamonds, was considered a modest alternative to the Imperial State Crown. Victoria wore it with a widow's veil for the State Opening of Parliament in 1871 and continued to wear it for state occasions until her death. Queen Alexandra and Queen Mary both wore this crown before it was put on display at the Tower of London in 1937.

89

Gold, diamond and silk velvet garter *(above right)* On her accession in 1837, when Victoria became Sovereign of all the British orders of chivalry, she needed a substantial amount of new insignia. That year, she had Rundell, Bridge & Co rework this garter from the diamond garter of her grandfather, George III, using 473 of the original 622 diamonds mounted on blue velvet. The motto of the Order of the Garter is written in diamonds: *'honi soit qui mal y pense'* ('shame upon him who thinks evil of it'). Victoria wore the garter around her upper left arm instead of below the left knee, where it was traditionally worn.

90

Mourning jewellery The Queen wore more restrained jewellery after Prince Albert's death. This sombre mourning ring *(top)* contains a microphotograph of Albert, made for her in *c*1861. Black jet accessories complemented her usual mourning attire. On 1 April 1867, the *Ladies Treasury* remarked 'at the court recently held by the Queen, Her Majesty wore a black silk dress, with a train trimmed round with crape, and the Mary Queen of Scots cap, with a long veil of white crape lisse, and a coronet of jet. HM also wore jet ornaments, the riband and Star of the Order of the Garter, and the Victoria and Albert Order'.

IN HER OWN WORDS...

Throughout her life Victoria spoke very directly and at times could be very wilful – characteristics that sometimes got her into trouble with her family, her ministers and her public.

91

'When you are naughty you make me and yourself very unhappy,' scolded the Duchess of Kent. 'No Mama, not *me*, not myself, but *you*!' was young Victoria's cheeky reply.

92

'I will be good.' On first being shown a chart of the line of succession at the age of 10, tipped into a book by her governess Baroness Lehzen. (11 March 1830)

93

Victoria recorded the day of her Coronation, 28 June 1838, in her diary in great, rather frank detail: [Lord Melbourne] 'kindly asked if I was tired; said the Sword he carried (the first, the Sword of State) was excessively heavy. I said that the Crown hurt me a good deal.'

My dearest Albert put on my stockings for me. I went in and saw him shave; a great delight for me

The Queen... will not submit to such trickery

94

At the start of her reign Victoria was challenged by the head of the Tory Opposition, Sir Robert Peel, over her choice of Ladies of the Bedchamber. She showed her strength of character to her mentor, the Prime Minister, Lord Melbourne: 'I was calm but very decided, and I think you would have been pleased to see my composure and great firmness: the Queen of England will not submit to such trickery. Keep yourself in readiness, for you may soon be wanted.' (9 May 1839)

95

'It was with some emotion...that I beheld Albert – who is beautiful.' Although theirs was an arranged marriage, Victoria was smitten with Albert from early on and deeply in love with him, which continued throughout their lives together. Three days after her wedding she wrote in her journal: 'My dearest Albert put on my stockings for me. I went in and saw him shave; a great delight for me'. 10 October 1839-13 February 1840.

96

When Victoria had her first child, 'Princess Vicky' on 21 November 1840 she was told by her doctor, 'Oh madam, it is a princess.' 'Never mind,' said the Queen, 'the next will be a Prince'.

97

'Lord John Russell may resign, and Lord Aberdeen [Prime Minister] may resign, but I can't resign. I sometimes wish I could.' Victoria's frustration with her ministers at the collapse of the Government (caused in part by Disraeli's criticism) at the beginning of the Crimean War.

98

On childbirth, writing to her daughter Vicky who was giving birth to the future Kaiser Wilhelm II in 1859: 'Poor dear darling! I pitied you so! It is indeed too hard and dreadful what we have to go through and men ought to have an adoration for one, and indeed do everything to make up, for what after all they alone are the cause of!'

99

When Prince Albert died on 14 December 1861, from what was then diagnosed as typhoid, Victoria was thrown into a period of inconsolable grief, from which she never truly recovered. She wrote to her Uncle Leopold: 'The poor fatherless baby of eight months is now the utterly broken-hearted and crushed widow of forty-two! My life as a happy one is ended! the world is gone for me!'

100

'Please understand that there is no one depressed in *this* house; we are not interested in the possibilities of defeat; they do not exist,' the Queen said to Arthur Balfour, minister in charge of the Foreign Office on the Boer War during 'Black Week', 10-15 December 1899.

> It is indeed too hard and too dreadful what we have to go through

VICTORIA THE WIFE, MOTHER AND WIDOW

Queen Victoria was struck by Prince Albert's beauty when she met her cousin for the second time in 1839 (they had first met at Kensington Palace in 1836). She quickly fell in love and they married in 1840. At first Albert struggled to carve his own niche in public life but he gradually gained influence at home. By 1845, he was advising the Queen on political decisions to such an extent that the diarist Charles Greville wrote: 'They are one person, and He likes and She dislikes business.' Victoria looked to Albert's tastes in music, art and literature. Together, they shared an ardent interest in raising and educating their nine children. The Queen never recovered fully from the shock of Albert's death in 1861. The once happy family birthdays and Christmases she described in her journals became painful reminders of Albert's absence. The image of the Queen in her 'widow's weeds' remains central to the popular understanding of her today.

ALBERT AND THE CHILDREN

Victoria and Albert's mutual affection and shared interests created a happy marriage and they produced nine children, many of whom eventually married into other European royal families earning Victoria the nickname the 'Grandmother of Europe'.

101

Albert, Prince of Saxe-Coburg and Gotha (Albert Francis Charles Augustus Emmanuel) (1819-61) Shortly after Victoria met her future husband she wrote: 'He possesses every quality that could be desired to render me perfectly happy. He is so sensible, so kind, and so good, and so amiable too. He has, besides, the most pleasing and delightful exterior and appearance you can possibly see.'

102

Victoria, Princess Royal (1840-1901) Known affectionately as 'Pussy', 'Pussette' or 'Vicky'. Described by her governess as 'all gracefulness and prettiness, very fat and active, running about and talking a great deal' but 'over sensitive' and temperamental. Her mother found her difficult and rebellious but her father delighted in her intelligence and extrovert ways.

103

Albert Edward, Prince of Wales (1841-1910) Known as 'Bertie' to his family. The young Prince lacked his elder sister's intelligence and struggled with his studies, much to the disappointment of his mother and father. After 59 years as heir apparent to the throne (a record only surpassed a century later by Charles, Prince of Wales), he finally acceded as King Edward VII in 1901.

104

Alice (1843-78) Victoria's second daughter was described by the Queen as 'a pretty and large baby…we think will be the beauty of the family'. Shortly after her 18th birthday she became engaged to Prince Louis of Hesse. Their wedding took place six months after the death of Prince Albert and, with the whole court in mourning, was described as 'the saddest royal wedding in modern times'.

105

Alfred (1844-1900) From a young age, the Queen's second son, known to his family as 'Affie', had a passion for all things nautical and at the age of 14 he entered the Royal Navy. His mother lamented his departure, saying it was 'much better to have no children than to have them only to give them up'.

Page 38: Queen Victoria by Brian Edward Duppa, 5 July 1854 (detail).

Previous page **Left:** An early photograph by Roger Fenton of the Queen with her four eldest children, (from left) Albert Edward, Victoria, Alice and Alfred. **Right:** this souvenir card opens to reveal a happy family scene.

This page **Left to right:** Louise, seated with Arthur (in tartan) and Leopold, painted by Franz Xaver Winterhalter in 1856; The delicate and academic Leopold, photographed *c*1865; Beatrice, painted by Winterhalter in 1859.

106

Helena (1846-1923) Known to her family as Lenchen (the German name for Helena was Helenchen, which means little Helen, shortened to Lenchen). The tomboy of the family, she was interested in engines and machines and enjoyed riding, running and boating. As a teenager she became romantically attached to her father's German librarian, Carl Ruland, who was promptly dismissed as soon as Victoria found out.

107

Louise (1848-1939) Princess Louise was a talented artist. Her marble statue of her mother at the time of her accession still stands outside Kensington Palace, where Louise lived with her husband. She was the only one of Victoria's children not to give her grandchildren.

108

Arthur, Duke of Connaught (1850-1942) Queen Victoria was particularly fond of her third son, writing of him, 'The Child is dear, dearer than any of the others put together'. At an early age, Arthur developed an interest in the army, playing for hours with his model soldiers and reading accounts of the Napoleonic Wars. He joined the British Army in 1868, where he served for some 40 years.

109

Leopold, Duke of Albany (1853-84) The Queen's youngest son was a haemophiliac

and was very delicate as a child, unable to join in the boisterous games of his brothers and sisters. Victoria didn't seem to like him as much as her other children and described him as 'a common-looking child, though amusing'.

110

Beatrice (1857-1944) Queen Victoria's ninth and last child was born a few weeks before her 38th birthday. Known as 'Baby' by her mother, she grew up in the shadow of the Queen's prolonged and intense mourning for Prince Albert who died when Beatrice was just 4. After her mother's death, Beatrice spent 30 years editing her journals – at the Queen's request. About a third of the original material was destroyed due to her censorship.

VICTORIA AND ALBERT

Victoria and Albert's marriage was built on genuine love and affection and an abundance of shared interests. They fell in love in 1839 and were married for 21 years. After Albert's death in 1861 the devoted Victoria continued to preserve his memory for the rest of her life.

111

A love match Relatives began plotting a match between Victoria and her German cousin when the couple were infants. 'The little fellow is the pendant to the pretty cousin', enthused their grandmother soon after Albert's birth. Victoria's Uncle Leopold was particularly keen on the pairing. He engineered their first meeting at Kensington Palace in 1836 against the King's wishes (William IV had other ideas for suitable bridegrooms).

112

Personal politics Victoria fell madly in love with Albert when he arrived at Windsor in 1839 and a few days later they were engaged. However, the young couple could not escape political considerations as they planned their future private lives. When Albert assumed he could choose his own staff, the Queen insisted he take the Whig Prime Minister's secretary into his Household. A tense exchange of letters between the couple revealed who was in charge, as Albert grudgingly complied with his future wife's instructions!

113

Official disapproval Parliament met the announcement of Queen Victoria's engagement to a penniless German prince with suspicion. Amid accusations that Albert was a Catholic, the ministers' flat refusal to grant him either a peerage or the King Consort title infuriated Victoria, who scrawled, 'I'll never forgive these infernal scoundrels!'

114

Developing Albert's role If Albert felt left out of the Queen's official duties at first, her pregnancy in 1840 helped the situation immeasurably. When she

Left to right: A highly romanticised Victoria and Albert in *The Honeymoon*, by Robert Hannah c1840; Royal wedding souvenir tins, each containing a slice of cake, were presented to guests; Victoria and Albert photographed by Roger Fenton after a reception at Buckingham Palace in 1854; Christmas engraving, 1848.

was not feeling up to it, he read her daily Government dispatches to her. As her pregnancy progressed, she had their desks at Buckingham Palace placed side-by-side so they could work together. By Christmas, he was so firmly entrenched in public affairs that she gave him his own key to the red leather dispatch boxes.

115

Christmas traditions Holidays and birthdays were marked with great excitement. Victoria and Albert celebrated Christmas the German way, with gifts arranged on tables under small Christmas trees decorated with candles, ribbons and paper chains. The fashion for Christmas trees caught on as scenes of royal domestic life appeared in the new illustrated papers. This engraving *(right)* from the *Illustrated London News* dated 23 December 1848, shows Victoria, Albert and their children celebrating a family Christmas at Windsor Castle in 1848.

Left: Victoria made this sketch of Prince Albert in 1840. **Below left:** *Evening at Balmoral; the stags brought home* by Carl Haag, 1853-4. **Right:** Commemorative medal and gold,turquoise and diamond ring, both showing Albert and Victoria on their wedding day, 10 February 1840. Royal jewellers Rundell, Bridge & Rundell made 72 of these rings, which were given to friends and relations. **Far right:** Sir Edwin Landseer's *Windsor Castle in Modern Times* shows the happy couple in the early 1840s with their first child. The Queen described the painting as 'most pleasing and cheerful'.

116

A shared passion The royal couple had developed their musical interests independently of one another but playing music together brought them enormous pleasure. They played and sang Albert's compositions together and often played duets on the piano. Felix Mendelssohn described a lively scene at Buckingham Palace when Albert performed with 'all the music sheets going all over the floor, and being picked up by the Queen'. (See also pages 26-7)

117

Daily life After breakfast, a brisk walk outdoors and a few hours of work, Victoria and Albert often spent time sketching or painting. Together they produced etchings of their children, pets, friends and home life. These informal images sparked a scandal in 1848, when Jasper Tomsett Judge, who viewed secret copies of the etchings from the assistant of a

printer in Windsor, published *A Descriptive Catalogue of the Royal Victoria and Albert Gallery of Etchings.* After a lengthy court battle the catalogues were destroyed.

118

Prince Albert's official role Albert's first forays into public life focussed on the Queen's work but he shaped his own public role based on his interests in music, art, science and education. He gave lectures on the abolition of slavery and in 1847 he became Chancellor of Cambridge University, where he revamped the curriculum. He laid so many foundation stones that *Punch* magazine dubbed him 'Prince of Bricklayers' but the enormous success of the Great Exhibition in 1851 brought him respect and admiration.

119

Parenthood Victoria and Albert took pride in their first child Princess Vicky, who was the image of Prince Albert, but viewed the Prince of Wales as a perpetual disappointment. He was lazy and had no aptitude for his studies. The 19-year-old Bertie's descent into 'vice and debauchery' – and the 'disgusting details' of his relationship with a music hall artist – distressed his parents. The Queen blamed Bertie for Albert's resulting insomnia, exhaustion and, ultimately, for his death. (See also Fact 151)

120

Albert's death During the last days of his illness as he succumbed to what was believed to be typhoid, Albert oscillated between bouts of delirium and moments of clarity, pacing from room to room and resting, listless, on his sofa. Even in this disturbed state of mind, he never forgot his deep love and affection for Victoria. He smiled at her, stroked her face and called her pet names – 'Fräuchen' (little woman) and 'gutes Weibchen' (excellent little wife) – as he always had.

BABY MEMENTOES

Victoria cherished objects from her own childhood and those used by her children when they were very small. She had numerous pieces of jewellery made to commemorate them; late photographs show her weighed down with items.

123

This gold and enamel brooch *(below)* was designed by Prince Albert in 1847 as a rather bizarre souvenir. The 'thistle' is Princess Vicky's first milk tooth, which Albert pulled out himself (presumably when it was already loose)!

121

As a new mother, Victoria was given a very unusual brooch in the shape of a teething stick *(not shown)*. A present from her own mother, it was made of gold and coral, traditionally associated with children.

122

Albert gave this pretty bracelet *(above)* with one coloured enamel heart, to Victoria on the birth of their first child Vicky. Later hearts were added when new children arrived, inscribed with their name and date of birth. Each heart contains a lock of the child's hair.

124

Victoria kept a tiny pair of kid gloves worn by the 'baby' of the family, her last child Princess Beatrice, when she was about 18 months old.

Bottom: (from left) Family in miniature, all the children painted age 4, Princess Victoria, Albert Edward, Alice, Alfred, Helena, Louise, Arthur, Leopold and Beatrice.

125

The Queen used the same bassinet (cradle) for all her babies. It was made in 1840 and lined with silk, silk net and Honiton lace, the same kind of Devon-manufactured lace that was used to decorate the Queen's wedding dress.

126

Victoria's first six children were all immortalised at the age of 4 in miniatures mounted on a bracelet *(bottom left)* made of enamel, pearls and human hair! The Queen added to the bracelet with each new child.

127

Adding the last three children would have made the bracelet too big to wear, so miniatures of Arthur, Leopold and Beatrice were put on a separate bracelet *(bottom right)*, each tiny painting this time fastened on a velvet band.

128

The Queen loved having marble sculptures made of her children's hands and feet. This is Princess Louise's arm *(left)*. Plaster casts were taken while the children slept; 14 different casts were made and are preserved on red velvet cushions.

129

These princely velvet slippers *(below)* with rabbit fur tops and tiny Prince of Wales feathers embroidered in silver were worn by an infant Prince Albert Edward, or 'Bertie'.

130

Victoria kept several of her children's christening gowns. A gorgeous dark blue silk velvet cloak trimmed with ermine, worn by the Princess Royal, is now in the Royal Ceremonial Dress Collection.

A contemplative Queen in this official Diamond Jubilee portrait by Lafayette in 1897.

VICTORIA'S SORROWS

During Queen Victoria's long life and reign she endured many personal sorrows including the death of numerous family members: her own children, her grandchildren and, the greatest sorrow of all, the death of her beloved Prince Albert.

131

In January 1844, the Queen's father-in-law, the Duke of Saxe-Coburg and Gotha, died after a short illness. Victoria – thinking of Albert and his loss – 'plunged into ecstasies of mourning': 'We feel crushed, overwhelmed, bowed down by the loss of one who was so desperately loved, I may say adored, by his children and family.' In reality the Duke had been a difficult man, and had badgered Victoria for money.

132

Victoria was overwhelmed by the death of her mother, the Duchess of Kent, in March 1861; so much so that her son, the Prince of Wales, is said to have found her grief 'excessive'.

133

Prince Albert died from what was thought to be typhoid fever on 14 December 1861, at the age of 42. The Queen was devoted to her husband and her grief was overwhelming. She wore black for the rest of her reign and for the next decade rarely appeared in public. Although she never neglected her official duties, she was widely criticised for living in seclusion.

134

In November 1878, Victoria's 4-year-old granddaughter, Princess May, daughter of Princess Alice, died from diphtheria. Her whole family was stricken with the disease and more bad news was soon to follow.

135

Still reeling from the death of her grand-daughter, Victoria was devastated to learn of the death of her own daughter Princess Alice in the following month. Alice's only son Ernest was gravely ill and she gave him what was later described as 'the kiss of death' – for her. Three days later Ernest was out of danger but Alice had caught the disease and died – aged 35 – on the 17th anniversary of Prince Albert's death.

We feel crushed, overwhelmed, bowed down by the loss of one who was so desperately loved

136

The Queen was left bereft by the death of John Brown, her personal servant and favourite, in March 1883. They had become close after Albert's death and the exact nature of their relationship was the subject of much speculation by contemporaries (and continues to be controversial today). After his death she wrote, 'The Queen feels that life for the second time is become most trying and sad to bear, deprived of all she so needs… the blow has fallen too heavily not to be very heavily felt.'

137

In March 1884, the Queen's son, Prince Leopold, died in the South of France. A haemophiliac, Leopold had gone to Cannes to escape the English winter. While there, he fell and injured his knee. The injury was accentuated by his haemophilia and caused an internal haemorrhage. He died two days later.

138

The Queen was very distressed to learn of the death of her grandson, Prince Albert Victor, Duke of Clarence, in January 1892. Albert, the eldest son of the Prince of Wales, was engaged to be married and with the wedding just a few weeks away, he developed pneumonia and died, aged 28.

139

The Queen's son-in-law, Prince Henry (who was married to her daughter Beatrice) died of malaria in 1896 while fighting in the Anglo-Asante War. Victoria wrote: 'The sorrow is overwhelming and to me is a double one, as I lose a dearly loved and helpful son, whose presence was like a sunbeam in my home, and my dear daughter loses a noble and devoted husband.'

140

In July 1900, Victoria's son, Alfred, died from throat cancer. The Queen wrote: 'It is a horrible year, nothing but sadness and horrors of one kind & another.'

VICTORIA'S MOST INTERESTING GRANDCHILDREN

Queen Victoria's 39 grandchildren formed the basis of a vast European family network, producing seven crowned heads and over a thousand descendants. By the birth of her 14th grandchild Victoria remarked wearily that 'it becomes a very uninteresting thing – for it seems to me to go on like the rabbits in Windsor Park'.

141

William II, King of Prussia, Emperor of Germany (1859-1941) 'Kaiser Bill' Victoria wrote in January 1859: 'I own it seems very funny to me to be a grandmama, and so many people tell me they can't believe it!' Her first grandchild would, she was sure, be a blessing to his country, but she eventually changed her opinion of the man who was to shape Europe's destiny in a very different way. Many years later, as the Queen's life ebbed, he rushed to Osborne from Germany, and she died in his arms.

142

Prince Francis Frederick Sigismund of Prussia (1864-66) Disease was to carry off several of Victoria's grandchildren. Little Prince Sigismund was his mother's favourite, a 'little sunbeam in the house' but he was also the first to die, aged just 22 months from meningitis, in June 1866.

143

Alexandra Feodorovna, Empress of Russia (1872-1918) The nervous and highly strung Alix of Hesse made a love-match with Nicholas II, Emperor of Russia. Deeply unpopular in her adopted country, domineering over her weak-willed husband and perceived as partly responsible for the Russian Revolution, her life was cruelly ended with her husband and their children in a hail of bullets.

144

Prince Albert Victor, Duke of Clarence (1864-92) In the fullness of time, 'Eddy' would have become king, but no prince has been so maligned by historians who have accused him of being a promiscuous homosexual, educationally sub-normal and even possibly Jack the Ripper. In fact Albert Victor was probably no more than lazy: 'an inveterate and incurable dawdler' as one of his relatives put it. He died of pneumonia at the age of 28.

145

Victoria Eugenie, Queen of Spain (1887-1969) 'Ena' was a beauty who caught the King of Spain's eye but

Left to right: 'Kaiser Bill' wearing his military uniform emblazoned with the totenkopf (death's head emblem); Tsarina Alexandra Feodorovna, *c*1894-5, with her four daughters, all executed by Bolsheviks at Ekaterinburg in 1918; Carnet with a miniature of the Tsarina; A bomb, thrown by an anarchist, explodes by the royal carriage on Victoria Eugenie's wedding day; Card celebrating the engagement of Victoria of Hesse and Prince Louis of Battenberg in 1884.

through her, the haemophilia gene was introduced to the Spanish royal family. Most famously, on the day of her marriage, an anarchist threw a bomb at the carriage. Her white wedding dress was spattered with an injured soldier's blood; an inauspicious start to a troubled reign.

146

Marie, Queen of Romania (1875-1938) The attractive young 'Missy' married Ferdinand, the Crown Prince of Romania; 'a very stupid young man with large protruding ears', in the words of one British diplomat. Though ambivalent towards her husband, she fell utterly in love with her adopted land.

147

Princess Victoria of Hesse and by Rhine (1863-1950) Orphaned like her sister Alix at a young age, the Princess was taken under the protective wing of her grandmother Queen Victoria, who advised her not to allow herself to be pushed into marriage. Victoria took her at her word and married a poor relation for love – Louis of Battenberg. Her own grandson is Prince Philip, Duke of Edinburgh.

148

Princess Marie Louise (1872-1956) Marie Louise was not the prettiest of Queen Victoria's grandchildren; when sent to stay with Grandmama, the Queen sent a telegraph to her parents: 'children very well, but poor little Louise very ugly'. When challenged, the Queen remarked 'my dear child, it was only the truth'.

149

Prince Maurice of Battenberg (1891-1914) Maurice was the last of Queen Victoria's grandchildren to be born, some 32 years after the first. Joining the King's Royal Rifle Corps at the outbreak of hostilities in 1914, he was killed almost straight away as the Queen's grandchildren went to war with one another.

150

Princess Alice, Countess of Athlone (1883-1981) After an active and public life Princess Alice, the daughter of the haemophiliac Prince Leopold was the last of Victoria's vast tribe of grandchildren to die, at the age of 97. With her, one of the last living links to the Victorian age disappeared.

PRIVATE LIVES

Victoria's family was portrayed in the press as ideal, with she and Albert proud parents of nine picture-perfect children. However, as adults, the royal offspring often fell short of the enthusiastically promoted public image.

151

The Prince of Wales became well known for his countless affairs. Albert Edward's first liaison, which scandalised his parents, was with a small-time actress, Nellie Clifden. Smuggled into the tent of the 20-year-old 'Bertie', who was camping with the army outside Dublin, Clifden made sure the story of her royal conquest was soon common knowledge in London society.

152

Victoria and Albert's eldest child, Princess Victoria, was famous for her lack of tact. Her deliberate championing of English traditions and promotion of her father's liberal views angered her German in-laws and much of Berlin society; she was known unfavourably as 'die Engländerin'.

153

Although a devoted nurse (she tended her father in his last hours and nursed her brother Bertie through serious illness), Princess Alice was inclined to talk with medical candour about gynaecological matters to her younger sisters, which infuriated Queen Victoria.

154

Prince Alfred was the sailor son, known for his heavy drinking, swearing and smoking. He caused further outrage by marrying a Russian princess, Grand Duchess Marie. (Anglo-Russian relations were far from warm and the Russian Orthodox Church was viewed with suspicion.)

155

The most placid of Victoria's daughters, Princess Helena, developed something of a drug habit in middle age. Like many Victorian women, she frequently took laudanum and opium, originally prescribed to help with minor illnesses.

156

Victoria's favourite son Prince Arthur was something of a golden boy within the family, happily married to Princess Louise of Prussia. However, this didn't stop him having a long term liaison with Léonie Leslie, the sister of Lady Randolph Churchill.

157

Constantly frustrated by his over-protective mother, the haemophiliac Prince Leopold was once so exasperated that he threatened to stand for parliament as an 'extreme radical'. As a result of this outburst Prime Minister Disraeli persuaded the Queen to use Leopold as a confidential secretary and he was given the keys to the government dispatch boxes (a privilege denied to his elder brother the Prince of Wales).

158

Victoria confidently expected the 'baby' of the family, Princess Beatrice, to stay by her side as a companion into her old age. There was a monumental showdown when Beatrice announced her intention to marry Prince Henry of Battenburg. For six months mother and daughter hardly spoke to each other, communicating by frosty notes. Eventually Victoria relented, after much cajoling from her family, but only on the condition that the young couple would remain with her.

159

Beautiful, artistic Princess Louise was never far from some minor scandal or gossip. Many believed her husband, the Marquess of Lorne, was homosexual and Louise compensated by an affair with her tutor, the sculptor Edward Boehm. When

Left to right: Butter wouldn't melt in the mouth of the young Albert Edward, painted in 1846 by Franz Xaver Winterhalter; Princes Louise, photographed in Venice in 1890; Bust of Gouramma, commissioned by the Queen from Carlo Marochetti, 1855.

her tutor died suddenly of a heart attack Louise was present in his studio.

160

When the 10-year-old Gouramma, daughter of deposed Coorg Rajah, arrived in England in 1851 to receive a European education she was presented to Queen Victoria. She aroused the interest of the matronly Queen, who grew immensely fond of her. The Indian Princess was baptised in 1852 at Buckingham Palace, taking the name of the Queen, with Victoria acting as one of the god-mothers.

VICTORIA THE SOVEREIGN

Victoria was just 18 years old when she became Queen in 1837. Still just a girl, she leaned heavily on her two most trusted advisers: her uncle Leopold and Lord Melbourne, the Prime Minister. Her early years on the throne were marred by scandals such as the Bedchamber Crisis (she refused to budge when the new Prime Minister Robert Peel demanded she replace some of her Ladies of the Bedchamber with wives of his Tory ministers) and the Flora Hastings Affair (see Fact 189) but Queen Victoria soon aimed to gain a greater respect for the monarchy. She took her duties so seriously that she allowed herself and Prince Albert only three days' honeymoon after their wedding. Victoria's personal likes and dislikes shaped her relationships with her ministers and her letters to them reveal a fiery temper. Her sharp withdrawal from public life after Prince Albert's death in 1861 was disastrous for her public image but the enormous Golden and Diamond Jubilee celebrations helped to restore her popularity. Still the country's longest reigning monarch, she ruled Britain and its sprawling empire for 63 years.

VICTORIA'S PRIME MINISTERS

Conveniently for this book, Victoria had ten Prime Ministers. Some of them occupied 10 Downing Street more than once in an age when politics was volatile and governments were short, but politicians lasted much longer.

161

William Lamb, 2nd Viscount Melbourne (1835-41) Victoria's first Prime Minister was a self-confessed bore, afflicted with what has been described as 'an incapacitating inertia and disinterest'. The young Queen hung on his every word, seeing him as a father-figure, and only her marriage to Albert broke her dependency on him.

162

Sir Robert Peel (1841-6) Beginning as a Tory and ending as a Conservative, Peel created a new party out of the ashes of the one he helped destroy over the repeal of the protectionist Corn Laws, Catholic emancipation, and parliamentary reform. He was in many areas a great if unexpected social and free trade reformer. The police force he founded took the nicknames 'Peelers' or 'Bobbies'. His activity in Ireland gave him the nickname (from the Protestant Order) 'Orange' Peel.

163

Lord John Russell (1846-52, 1865-6) The short and scrawny 'Finality Jack' was, in the words of the Queen, 'a dreadful old man', who was interested in 'nothing except the Constitution of 1688 and himself'. He had to contend with the famine in Ireland and agitation by Chartists but he had been a reformer in the early 1830s and his attempts to alleviate suffering and improve society continued through his ministries.

164

Edward Smith-Stanley, 14th Earl of Derby (1852, 1858-9, 1866-8) The Irish patriot Daniel O'Connell called him 'Derby Dilly', while Victoria herself complained that he was the 'most difficult and unsatisfactory minister she or indeed anyone had to deal with'. Serving three short terms of less than two years each, Lord Derby did manage to establish a system of national schools in Ireland.

165

George Hamilton-Gordon, 4th Earl of Aberdeen (1852-5) The mild mannered and pacifist Aberdeen had the misfortune to be raised to office on the eve of the Crimean War after Lord John Russell's resignation (see Fact 97). The Queen remembered him fondly: 'One of the few remaining experienced and truly loyal public men, who would never tolerate any dis-honourable proceedings, straight-forward, high minded, the kindest of friends, so wise in his opinions.'

166

Henry John Temple, 3rd Viscount Palmerston (1855-8, 1859-65) 'Pam' the arch-imperialist was never afraid of interfering, sending in the gun-boats to exert Britain's will on a reluctant world. 'We had', said the Queen, 'God knows! terrible trouble with him about Foreign Affairs'. By the time of his last ministry, he was deaf, dyed his hair and, as one commentator noted, had 'false

Previous page: Queen Victoria by Franz Xaver Winterhalter, 1856.

This page **Left to right:** William Lamb 2nd Viscount Melbourne by Sir Thomas Lawrence; Visual pun of Robert Peel, depicting him as a bell; *An Omnibus Ride to Piccadilly Circus, Mr Gladstone Travelling with Ordinary Passengers* painted by Alfred Morgan 1885; Queen Victoria with 'Dizzy' Disraeli at his home, Hughenden Manor.

teeth which would fall out of his mouth when speaking if he did not hesitate and halt so much in his talk'. But in other ways, his vigour never diminished and in those jingoistic days he remained enormously popular.

167

Benjamin Disraeli (1868, 1874-80) 'I have', he noted on becoming Prime Minister, 'climbed to the top of the greasy pole'. His flattery, especially of Victoria, was legendary, and she was utterly susceptible. One of the best known politicians of the era, 'Dizzy' also had a successful literary career, and his track record in reforms included public health and improvements in factories.

168

William Ewart Gladstone (1868-74, 1880-5, 1886, 1892-4) Gladstone the 'great liberator' harboured an intense rivalry with Disraeli, while the Queen complained that he addressed her like a public meeting. With a career lasting over 60 years, four times in office, his reforms were far-reaching and have lasted to the present day, but his greatest cause, Home Rule in Ireland, was thwarted by a parliament not yet ready for such a radical shift. In 1897, not long before he died, he met the Queen at Cannes. After 50 years of frostiness, she had finally softened enough to shake his hand for the first time.

169

Archibald Primrose, 5th Earl of Rosebery (1894-5) At first, Rosebery was 'quite the rising politician of the day and is always very respectful and anxious to please me', wrote Victoria, but he later became disillusioned with politics and what he saw as democratic tyranny. Privately he confided that only two people were said to have ever frightened him: Bismarck and Queen Victoria.

170

Robert Gascoyne-Cecil, 3rd Marquess of Salisbury (1885-6, 1886-92, 1895-1902) Queen Victoria's last Prime Minister enjoyed a warm relationship with her. Lord Salisbury's daughter observed: 'I never saw two people get on better, their polished manners and deference to and esteem for each other were a delightful sight and not one readily to be forgotten'. His expertise was in foreign affairs; he represented the culmination of imperial power, promoting the doctrine of 'splendid isolation'. 'English policy', he said, 'is to float lazily downstream, occasionally putting out a diplomatic boathook to avoid collisions'.

THE CORONATION AND OTHER EVENTS

The coronation is arguably the single most important day of a monarch's life, and Victoria's on 28 June 1838 was a memorable affair, although not without a few embarrassing glitches.

171

Victoria's coronation cost a total of £69,421 – a mere snip when compared to the crowning of her uncle George IV in 1821, which cost £238,000. It was still impressive: Victoria's coronation robes included a cloth of gold robe brocaded with emblems of the United Kingdom.

172

In her journal, Victoria described every detail of her coronation, not sparing anyone's blushes. During the Homage 'poor old Lord Rolle, who is 82 and dreadfully infirm, when attempting to ascend the steps, fell and rolled quite down, but was not at the least hurt'.

173

Her Prime Minister Lord Melbourne told her afterwards, 'you did it beautifully – every part of it, with so much taste; it's a thing that you can't give a person advice upon; it must be left to a person'.

174

However, Benjamin Disraeli, who was then a Member of Parliament for the borough of Maidstone, remarked on a 'want of rehearsal' for the coronation. As he wrote to his sister, 'Melbourne looked very awkward and uncouth, with his coronet cocked over his nose, his robes under his feet, and holding the great Sword of State like a butcher.'

175

Much of the existing coronation regalia had to be re-made or altered to suit Victoria's small stature. Her coronation ring was new, a smaller version of her uncle William IV's, although due to a misunderstanding the royal jewellers actually made it too small! During the ceremony, the Archbishop of Canterbury had to force it onto her finger. She later wrote in her journal: 'I had the greatest difficulty to take it off again – which at last I did with great pain.'

Other key events...

176

The Great Exhibition, 1851 Albert had played a key role in organising this huge project and Victoria expressed great pride in her husband's achievement. (See also pages 116-19)

177

Victoria's retreat into mourning Just three weeks after her beloved Albert's death in 1861, Victoria held a Privy Council meeting. She was so grief-stricken she could not utter a word. The Council met in Albert's room, while the Queen remained in her adjacent room with the door open. She later wrote: 'the business was all summed up in two paragraphs, and Mr. Helps read "approved" for me. This was unlike anything that had been done before.' The event marked the start of Victoria's withdrawal into prolonged mourning.

Left: The coronation procession of Queen Victoria to Westminster Abbey, 1838. This was mass-produced as a street souvenir, with 30 hand coloured-sections.
Right: *The Coronation of Queen Victoria* by Edmund Thomas Paris, 1838.

Celebrations in Trafalgar Square marking Victoria's Golden Jubilee, by Dudley Hardy, 1887. **Right:** Victoria's funeral cortège passing through the streets of London, 1901.

178

The Golden Jubilee 1887 Great excitement surrounded the celebrations in June and brought renewed vigour to the Queen's image, damaged after she had retreated from public view following Albert's death. She was impressed by the crowds but could not forget her private grief: 'The day has come, and I am alone.'

179

The Diamond Jubilee 1897 Before leaving Buckingham Palace for the Jubilee procession on 22 June, Victoria sent a telegraph message to the world thanking her subjects for their loyalty. It read: 'From my heart I thank my beloved people. May God bless them!' She received thousands of congratulatory messages from all over the world.

180

Victoria's funeral This enormous state event took place 11 days after her death at Osborne House on 22 January 1901. The Queen's body was brought back by train to London, and crowds lined the streets as her funeral cortège passed by on its way to St George's Chapel, Windsor. On a very personal level, Victoria had left discreet instructions for certain items to be placed beside her in her coffin. The Queen's doctor, Sir James Reid oversaw the final preparations of her body and placed with her 'rings, chains, bracelets, lockets, photographs, shawls, handkerchiefs, casts of hands' and Albert's dressing gown. Finally, in accordance with her wishes, Reid secreted in her hand under a posy of flowers a photograph of John Brown and a lock of his hair.

TEN KEY MEMBERS OF STAFF

Although Victoria became deeply attached to several of her ladies-in-waiting, we know little about most of the Queen's servants, many of whose names Princess Beatrice deleted when she edited and transcribed her mother's journals after her death in 1901.

181

John Brown Personal ghillie to the Prince Consort from 1858. Brown gained a more central role in the Queen's household after Albert's death in 1861. He was a hard-drinking, irreverent Scot who, unlike most servants, refused to stand on ceremony for the Queen. The close friendship they developed invited salacious gossip about the precise nature of their relationship.

182

Baroness Louise Lehzen Victoria's governess from early childhood. Lehzen retained a profound influence over the Queen even after her marriage in 1840. Their close relationship began to spark arguments between Victoria and Albert – who viewed Lehzen as an interfering, manipulative gossip. She resisted his attempts to force her out but the Queen eventually released her from service in 1842.

183

Lieutenant Colonel Sir Arthur Bigge, 1st Baron Stamfordham Private Secretary to the Queen from 1895 until her death in 1901. When her eyesight began to fail, devoted Bigge copied all the Queen's correspondence in thick black ink so that she could still read it, despite the advent of typewriters. Bigge's reputation for showing the utmost discretion earned him the nickname 'Better NOT'.

184

The Munshi (Hafiz Abdul Karim). One of two Indian servants who joined the Queen's household in 1887, Abdul Karim's basic role soon expanded to Munshi (teacher). He gave the Queen lessons in Hindustani, taught her about Indian culture and helped with official Indian affairs.

Left to right: (top) John Brown in the early 1880s; Sir James Clark in 1860; Abdul Karim with the Queen in 1893; The unfortunate Flora Hastings, by William Findon 1840; Lady Lyttleton, from a study by John Jackson.

185

Sir James Clark Physician-in-Ordinary to the Queen from 1837 to 1860. It is surprising that Clark remained in post for so long, considering the diagnostic mistakes he made. During Albert's illness in 1861, he told the Queen there was no need to worry. The Prince died just a few days later.

186

The Duchess of Sutherland (Lady Leveson-Gower), Mistress of the Robes from 1837. The beautiful, statuesque and fashionable granddaughter of Georgiana, Duchess of Devonshire attended the Queen on her coronation and wedding days. At times, the Queen became a little jealous of Sutherland's close relationship with her beloved Prime Minister, Lord Melbourne. Nevertheless, they remained friends.

187

Lady Lyttleton (Sarah Spencer). Lady Superintendent of the Royal Nursery. Appointed shortly after the birth of the Prince of Wales, Lady Sarah supervised the royal children's diet, health, general wellbeing and selected the clothes they wore. Her close consultation on all nursery matters with the Queen and Prince Albert reveals their unusually deep involvement in their children's lives.

188

Sir James Reid On 16 January 1901, Sir James examined the Queen in her own bed for the first time. He had been Physician-in-Ordinary since 1881 but strict protocol barred any close physical contact with his royal patient. After her death six days later, Reid followed the secret instructions she had given him: he placed the jewellery, photographs, garments and other personal items in the coffin next to her body. (See also Fact 180)

189

Lady Flora Hastings, Lady-in-Waiting to the Duchess of Kent. Lady Flora complained of a swollen abdomen in 1839 and the royal doctor Sir James Clark wrongly concluded she was pregnant. Victoria rashly accused her of having an affair with Sir John Conroy, adding to her distress and stoking gossip. When poor Lady Flora died on 5 July a post mortem revealed her 'pregnancy' was a huge tumour. The young Queen was hissed and booed by crowds outside Buckingham Palace, and the Flora Hastings Affair became a memorable low point in the Queen's popularity.

190

Mary Bettans This dressmaker was based in London's Jermyn Street and supplied Princess Victoria's dresses from 1824. Although no precise records survive, she probably also made the young Queen's wedding dress in 1840. A book of fabric cuttings from her workshop, which survives at the Museum of London, offers a glimpse into the Queen's early wardrobe, which included many brightly-coloured, floral silks.

TEN CAUSES VICTORIA SUPPORTED

Victoria's reign spanned a time of both huge social depredation but also great reforms and improvements. The Queen was generous in lending her name – and often her private purse – to causes that appealed to her philanthropic nature.

191

In 1840 Victoria relinquished much of the royal pleasure grounds at Kew to form the Royal Botanic Gardens as a public garden and research institution. At the time this pioneering garden for the study of plants was in danger of being broken up and her gesture, coming with the arrival of director Sir William Hooker, probably saved Kew Gardens.

192

The once-thriving silk industry in east London's Spitalfields was in severe decline. In an attempt to attract further work for impoverished silk weavers, the Queen agreed to the publication of a souvenir album after her very theatrical Bal Costumé at Buckingham Palace, on 12 May 1842. (See also Fact 78)

193

In 1846, one of the worst years of the Irish potato famine, the British government took a harsh view on supporting the starving Irish and help was left to private charity. Victoria was called the 'Famine Queen' for supposedly only giving £5. In fact, she gave £2,000 of her own money to a famine relief fund set up by businessmen.

194

During the outburst of racism following the Indian Mutiny of 1857, the Queen agreed with the more tolerant Charles 'Clemency' Canning, Governor-General of India. She told him that Indians should know that 'there is no hatred to a brown skin'. She displayed real commitment to this modern attitude by befriending several Indians in her service.

195

During the Crimean War of 1853-6, Victoria was impressed to read of the medical reforms made by Florence Nightingale in her field hospital at Scutari. After the war

Opposite page **Left:** The Palm House at Kew, built between 1846 and 1848. **Top right:** *Queen Victoria's First Visit to her Wounded Soldiers* by Jerry Barrett, 1856. **Bottom right:** Florence Nightingale *c*1885. This page **Top:** The Victoria Cross. **Below:** Souvenir chocolate tin from 1899.

she presented Nightingale with a brooch to show her support. The Queen also visited wounded and ill soldiers and founded a new hospital for their care. (See also Fact 356)

196

The Crimean War also caused Victoria to inspire her undoubtedly brave soldiers by introducing the Crimea Campaign medal and then the celebrated Victoria Cross medal 'For valour' – the highest military decoration for bravery. This poignant inscription was Victoria's own suggestion. To this day, the medals are made from bronze recovered from Russian cannon captured at Sebastopol.

197

On 29 March 1871 Queen Victoria opened London's huge auditorium, the Royal Albert Hall. This 7,000-seater hall, inspired by the Roman Colosseum, was the centrepiece of what became known as Albertopolis, a grand scheme of Prince Albert's to create a great cultural citadel in South Kensington, including museums, for the education of the masses.

198

The Queen gave her royal patronage to the Royal Association in aid of the Deaf and Dumb (now Action on Hearing Loss) in 1873. That year, the new St Saviour's Church in London's Oxford Street became the first to offer sign language to encourage deaf worshippers.

199

In an age characterised by the importance of the home and family, it comes as no surprise that Victoria became patron of the Mothers' Union following her Diamond Jubilee year of 1897. The union had been founded some years before by rector's wife, Mary Sumner.

200

Concerned about troop morale during the second Boer War, in the winter of 1899 Victoria took up the suggestion of sending treats for Christmas. Three leading chocolate manufacturers were commanded to supply 120,000 special tins of chocolate (see example below from the Science Museum) to send to southern Africa. Sadly, many of the souvenir tins were later used to send home the personal effects of men who died during the campaign.

TEN OF VICTORIA'S 'LITTLE' WARS

Wars became an inevitable consequence of Britain's burgeoning expansion. 'If we are to maintain our position as a first-rate power', the Queen wrote, 'we must, with our Indian Empire and large Colonies, be prepared for attacks and wars, somewhere or other, CONTINUALLY'.

201

Asante Wars 1863-74 There were four Asante Wars in what is now the West African state of Ghana, with a fifth, final conflict known as the War of the Golden Stool, fought in 1900. They began with the British protecting their commercial interests, and ended with outright annexation of the Gold Coast to prevent the predatory French and Germans from taking over.

202

Opium Wars 1839-42, 1856-60 Gladstone called the opium trade a national disgrace. British, American and French merchants deliberately attempted to redress a trade imbalance by producing opium in India and flooding China with it. The results were prolonged conflict and the 'unequal treaties'. Britain's most conspicuous prize was Hong Kong.

Left: *The Relief of the Light Brigade* by Richard Caton Woodville, 1897, shows the survivors of the infamous Charge finally engaging the enemy. **Below:** Ex-officers of the Crimean War, taken from *Crimean Heroes*, an album of 26 photographs commissioned by Queen Victoria in 1856.

Over page **Main image:** A fearsome advance by Zulu troops, 1879, from an English newspaper. **Right:** Good news, the relief of Mafeking, South Africa, is announced in 1900. This famous action in the Boer War made a national hero of Robert Baden-Powell, who went on to found the Scout movement.

203

Crimean War 1853-6 The British and the French put their age-old differences behind them to take on Russia's might and check its expansionist tendencies into the Ottoman Empire. Most action took place in the Crimea on the Black Sea. A war known for its tactical and logistical errors, it was also famous for using technological novelties such as the telegraph, for the nursing innovations of Florence Nightingale and the birth of modern war journalism. The cavalry charge of the Light Brigade on 25 October 1854 has entered folklore as an example of heroic but deadly wrong-headedness.

204

Indian Mutiny 1857 For the British, this destructive war was a mutiny; for Indians, it is now seen as a war of independence. Control of India had grown piecemeal under the East India Company into a baffling mosaic of protectorates, trading bases and private territories. Rumblings of discontent grew until, unable to cope with widespread unrest, the Company was overwhelmed. In the bloody aftermath Britain assumed direct rule of the whole sub-continent.

205

Anglo-Satsuma War 1863 For Britain a mere skirmish and a footnote in history, but for the Japanese, the Anglo-Satsuma War, in which the British shelled the port of Kagoshima in an attempt to force Japan to trade, was part of a struggle to remain free of European colonisation.

206

The Abyssinian Expedition 1868 Sir Robert Napier led an expedition against the Emperor Theodore of Ethiopia after he had imprisoned British missionaries and diplomats. The Emperor had probably suffered a nervous breakdown some years before, and his defeat was followed by suicide, ironically with a pistol that Queen Victoria had sent him as a gift.

207

Second Afghan War 1878-80 Afghanistan is known as the graveyard of empires, and it was the place where British power met its match. Britain interfered in response to Russian expansionism, and ultimately the country was brought under a limited form of protection, but always at arm's length.

208

Zulu Wars 1879 In their expansion from the Cape of Good Hope, the British came into conflict with the powerful Zulu nation, led by King Ceteshwayo. A series of skirmishes culminated in the Battle of Isandlwana in 1879, when a British force was annihilated by Zulu warriors armed only with spears. The British finally deposed Ceteshwayo, who was exiled to London, where he met Queen Victoria!

209

Anglo-Zanzibar War 1896 The shortest war in history lasting just 38 minutes was precipitated by the death of the pro-British Sultan. As the new Sultan was not to their liking, the Royal Navy bombarded the royal palace on 27 August 1896 and installed a new sultan more favourable to their interests just over half an hour later.

210

Second Boer War 1899-1902 Queen Victoria's reign ended with a war in which the cracks in the imperial edifice began to show. British imperialists like Cecil Rhodes coveted the gold-and diamond-rich Boer Republics of Transvaal and Orange Free State. The cost of annexation was high; this was a war fought with guerrilla tactics and the shame of disease-ridden 'concentration' camps, where wives and children of Boer guerillas were sent and many perished. The result was deep and long-lasting bitterness towards Britain and widespread criticism throughout the world. Worry over the war may have hastened Queen Victoria's end.

VICTORIA'S WORLD

Queen Victoria lived in a world marked by radical and unprecedented change. By the end of her reign, colonial expansion, industrial production and new technologies had transformed the way people viewed the world, how they communicated with one another and how they moved from place to place. Photography, postage stamps, sewing machines, railways, pasteurisation, the bicycle, hydro-electric power, surgical anaesthetics and moving film are just some of the period's new developments. Victoria embraced many of these advances. She enthused about the telegraph machine demonstration she had seen at the Great Exhibition in 1851, tried chloroform to ease labour pains during the birth of two of her children and made a voice recording in 1888. The British Empire stretched across Africa, Asia, Australia and Canada. The growth of Victoria's family echoed this change. Her children had married into the royal houses of Europe and, empire-like, the family spread, earning her the title 'Grand-mother of Europe'.

POSTAGE

H ONE PENNY. H

TEN GREAT FEATS OF ENGINEERING

Victoria's reign ushered in an era of legendary construction, from the network of railways to thousands of miles of sewers, great bridges and monumental buildings.

211

The Great Western Railway (completed) 1841 Isambard Kingdom Brunel became Chief Engineer of the Great Western Railway in 1833, and immediately began work on a line to connect London to Bristol. He pioneered the 'broad gauge' track that enabled faster speeds. Many awe-inspiring viaducts and bridges were constructed on the network, including the Royal Albert Bridge at Saltash and the Maidenhead Bridge across the Thames - at the time the longest stretch of railway track over water.

212

Skerryvore Lighthouse (completed) 1844 The astonishingly difficult task to transport men, materials and tools to build this lighthouse on a huge Scottish rock, south of the Hebrides and surrounded by seas of legendary wildness, was directed by engineer Alan Stevenson in 1838 and completed by his younger brother Thomas in 1844. Over 30 men, working 17-hour days in summer months, finally built what is still the tallest lighthouse in Britain at over 47.5m (156ft).

213

The first steamship liner was built by Brunel in Bristol docks. The ss *Great Britain* was the first-ever iron-hulled luxury ocean steamship liner and was launched by Prince Albert in 1843. Her massive, rapid six-bladed screw

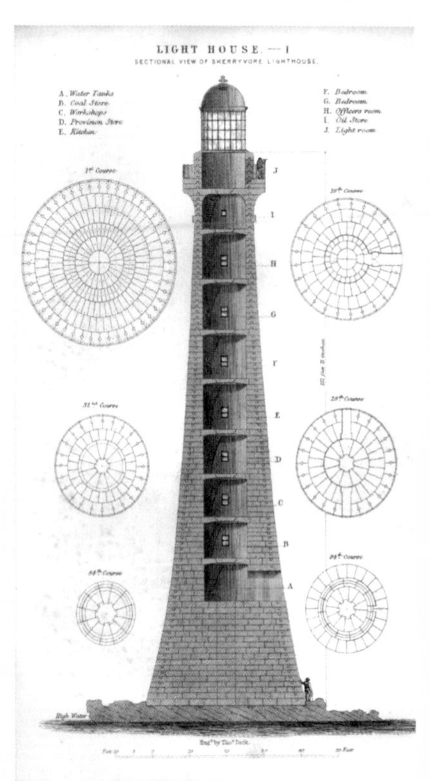

Previous page: The iconic Penny Black, the world's first adhesive stamp, issued 1 May 1843. The design was based on an engraving by William Wyon, taken from his bust of Princess Victoria modelled in 1834 when she was 15. This 'Young Head' design was also used on Victoria's coinage from 1838.

This page **Left to right:** Historical illustration of Skerryvore Lighthouse; Isambard Kingdom Brunel in front of the launching chains for his steamship the Great Eastern in 1857; *The Launch of the ss Great Britain* in July 1843, by Joseph Walter; Joseph Bazelgette, 1887.

propellers were a technological first, powering her across the Atlantic on her maiden voyage. Now she sits in Bristol's Great Western Dockyard: well worth a visit!

214

Britannia Tubular Bridge 1850

This bridge built over the Menai Straits used iron tubes supported by two box girders. Designed by Robert Stephenson, the structure could carry heavy loads without the need of suspension cables.

215

The Palace of Westminster

The Tsar of Russia called it 'a dream in stone' when he saw it, but Parliament's carved angels and Gothic pinnacles hide the most innovative and advanced building of its age, designed and built by Sir Charles Barry between 1840 and 1845. The building is constructed mostly of iron and concrete, and was designed to be fireproof (after the last one burned down) and centrally heated. Worn out by the project and all its complications, Barry lived just long enough to see its enduring icon, the tower that today we call 'Big Ben'.

216

A cure for the 'Great Stink' The five enormous sewers built under London between 1858 and 1870 by chief engineer Joseph Bazelgette and others played a vital role in protecting Londoners from waterborne disease, chiefly cholera. (See Fact 459)

217

The London Underground railway Although Americans can claim the first underground railway (New York, 1844), London was the first city to open a steam-powered, single line, multi-station system in 1863, designed by John Fowles. The Metropolitan line came first and proved a roaring success for Londoners, so that the network of tunnels expanded rapidly.

218

Clifton Suspension Bridge (completed) 1864 The first suspension bridge ever constructed, total length 412m (700ft) across the River Avon between Clifton on the Bristol side and Leigh Woods in Somerset. Brunel was just 24 when he won the commission in 1831, but construction took so long that he didn't live to see it finally opened.

Left to right: William Ewart Gladstone opens the Metropolitan Railway, London 1863; Clifton Suspension Bridge, photographed c1890; An 1887 demonstration of the structural principles of a cantilever bridge, with Sir John Fowler and Benjamin Baker, who designed the Forth Rail Bridge as the supports. The central 'weight' is provided by Kaichi Watanabe, one of the first Japanese engineers to study in Britain.

219

Forth Rail Bridge Designed by Benjamin Baker and completed in 1890, the massive mile-long rail bridge near Edinburgh was an engineering triumph of its time. The cantilever bridge (where the weight of the central span is transmitted to the banks) connects Edinburgh with Fife, and remains a major artery between the north east and south east of Scotland. It was one of the first major railroad bridges to use steel and, until the opening of the Quebec Bridge in 1918, the world's longest span.

220

And one failure... **the Tay Bridge** Opened in 1878 as the longest in the world, this bridge won engineer Thomas Bouch a knighthood from the Queen, who was delighted that her journey time to Balmoral would be reduced. However, the bridge, spanning over two miles across the Firth of Tay, had overreached itself. Disaster struck only a year later on 8 December 1879, when the central span collapsed under the 17.20 passenger train from Burntisland to Dundee. Seventy-five people died as engine and carriages plunged into the freezing water.

TEN CLASSIC NOVELS

During Victoria's reign the novel came into its own as a popular form of fiction, covering everything from social ills to religious doubt.

221

Jane Eyre by Charlotte Bronte (1847). Love conquers the social divide when our governess heroine finally wins her brooding hero – with a harrowing school experience, an attempt at bigamy and a madwoman in the attic thrown in for good measure.

222

Vanity Fair: A Novel without a Hero by William Makepeace Thackeray (1847-8). Thackeray charts the lives of individuals caught up in the Battle of Waterloo, satirising their all-too-human weaknesses and charting their fortunes, most notably in the character of the scheming, self serving anti-heroine Becky Sharp.

HARD TIMES.

223

Hard Times by Charles Dickens (1854). The industrial revolution brought unknown prosperity to Britain as a nation. However, this portrait of the manufacturing Coketown, 'where Nature was as strongly bricked out as killing airs and gases were bricked in', from the master story-teller of the 19th century, vividly demonstrated the misery and hardship it created.

224

The Daisy Chain or *Aspirations* by Charlotte M Yonge (1856). Though almost forgotten today, in the 19th century Yonge was a widely read author of some 160 books. *The Daisy Chain*, about the trials and tribulations of the May family, with its entirely Victorian blend of religion, education and redemption, was one of Yonge's most popular novels.

225

The Woman in White by Wilkie Collins (1860) One of the most popular novels of the 19th century, this was the first great sensation novel so beloved by the Victorians. With a twisting, engrossing plot involving insanity, jealousy and guilty secrets, it contains the brilliantly drawn villain Count Fosco, magnificent in his deviousness.

226

Alice's Adventures in Wonderland by Lewis Carroll (1865). With its white rabbit, red queen and clever nonsense this book broke the rules for children's literature (and appealed to many adults too). Instead of being about right or wrong, as was much of Victorian literature, it was just wonderfully strange, intriguing and fun.

227

Middlemarch by George Eliot (1874). Writer Mary Ann Evans used a male pen name in order to be taken seriously in an era when female novelists were usually associated with romantic fiction. This great novel of self-discovery, with its intricate cast of characters all struggling to find their place in life, was set in a provincial town at the time of the Great Reform Act.

Left to right: Charles Dickens photographed in 1870; an illustration from his novel *Hard Times*, 1854, of the fearsome Thomas Gradgrind and children Louisa and Tom; George Eliot, from an etching by Rajon after Frederick Burton; Arthur Rackham's depiction of the Mad Hatter's Tea Party from the 1907 edition of *Alice's Adventures in Wonderland*.

228

Tess of the D'Ubervilles by Thomas Hardy (1891). Set against a backdrop of rural transition, *Tess* is a very bleak love story that tackled head-on the seduction, abandonment and single motherhood of its eponymous heroine.

229

The Strange Case of Dr Jekyll and Mr Hyde by Robert Louis Stevenson (1886). Turned into a stage play within a year of its publication, this tale of split personality strongly appealed to Victorian readers eager for sensation and mystery.

230

Heart of Darkness by Joseph Conrad (1899). Written two years before Victoria's death Conrad's deeply unsettling work with its portrayal of slavery, brutality and cannibalism exposed the dark side of colonial imperialism.

TEN ASPECTS FROM 'THE DARK SIDE'

Grinding poverty, greed, exploitation or sheer desperation brought out the worst in Victoria's people, despite a system of harsh retributive punishment. Murder, rape, prostitution, theft, public disorder, rampant beggary, terrorism: all were part and parcel of Britain's frenetic development.

231

The sweated trades A great section of Victorian industry was based on child labour; a necessity for the poorest families. Even after the introduction of compulsory schooling, children were often taken out of school and put to work by desperate parents.

232

18 Cleveland Street Telegraph delivery boys caught playing with gold sovereigns in 1889 were accused of theft, until investigation uncovered a terrible scandal involving sodomy, aristocratic gentlemen including a royal equerry and shenanigans too scandalous to describe.

233

Dross puffers Charles Dickens captured the essence of England's opium dens in the opening of his novel *Edwin Drood*; of dingy, smoky rooms stuffed with the stupefied dregs of society. Opium, considered a 'pernicious luxury' or a national scourge, was just one aspect of a society in the throes of discovering 'new' drugs.

234

Baby farmers Margaret Waters promised desperate young unmarried mothers that she could find new and loving homes for their children, for a fee of £10. Then numerous tiny corpses were found washed up on the banks of the Thames. Though Waters was convicted and executed in 1870, a deeply troubling aspect of society was exposed publicly.

235

Mudlarks The Thames was one of the great shipping routes of the world, and the many barges plying the waters to unload cargo from the big ships were prey to an army of urchins, who would crawl aboard stealing anything of value and giving a helping hand to the illicit smuggling of tobacco and alcohol.

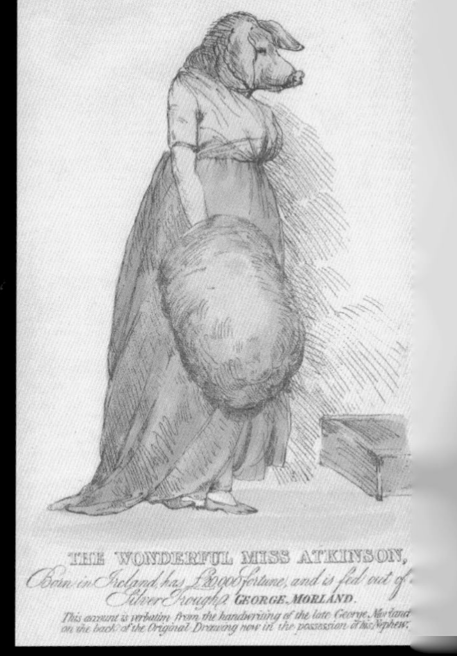

236

The pipe-smoking oyster Travelling freak shows and exhibitions throughout Europe and America provided low-brow entertainment reminiscent of an earlier age. These grisly shows advertised cannibal pygmies, spotted boys, Snake man, Hairy Mary, the Hottentot Venus, Miss Scott the Two-headed Lady, Jack the living skeleton and the immortal Elephan Man. Some were found wanting. Miss Stevens, the 18-year-old Pig-Faced Lady from Lancashire was, on closer inspectior discovered to be a bear in crinoline with her paws and faced shaved.

Left to right: Annie Jones, bearded lady with P T Barnum's circus, 1895; Conjoined twins Millie-Christine, who could sing (and no doubt harmonise) beautifully, 1875; The Enon Chapel, 'Cemetery and Dancing Saloon', featured in the *Poor Man's Guardian*, 1847

237

Warm gems Saucy novels with titles like *Lady Bumtickler's Revels* and erotic prints had been commonplace 'under the counter' material since the 18th century, but the invention of photography revolutionised pornography and created a whole new market. French imports were sold at extortionate rates. One anonymous vendor lured his customers with promises of 'rich and fast scenes from the Bagnios of Paris', and 'warm gems' which had to be seen to be appreciated. Police raids and the attentions of the Vice Society soon often followed.

238

Patter sellers Public execution was seen as a great day out in the early 19th century; even the railway companies laid on special trains and the hangman sometimes provided additional entertainment by spinning the corpse or jumping on the shoulders to snap the neck. Boys, described as 'an astonishing collection of ragamuffins and tatterdemalions, greasy, grimy and verminous' would sell penny pamphlets, describing the condemned's last moments to an eager, voyeuristic public. Public execution was abolished in 1868.

239

Prima donnas and dollymops Neither ballerinas nor cleaning utensils, but types of prostitute, who numbered perhaps 80,000 in London in the 1850s. 'Priestesses of Venus' could be socially mobile; some managed to marry into high society, but for most it was an escape from grinding poverty or a job on the side when work was scarce. At the bottom of the hierarchy were 'park women' who would offer soldiers a quick poke for a few coppers against a wall or in a dark alleyway.

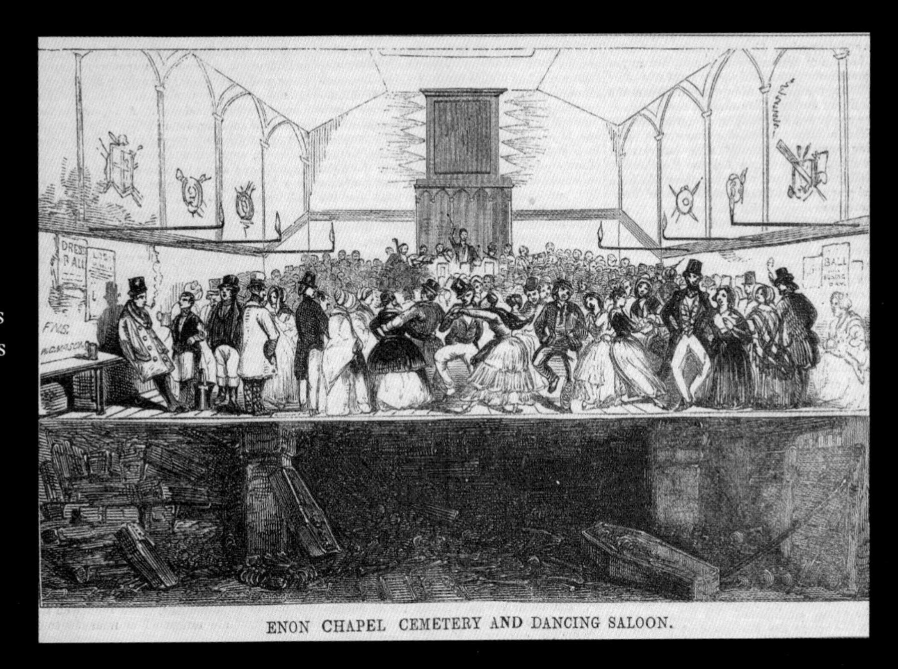

ENON CHAPEL CEMETERY AND DANCING SALOON.

240

The penny gaff The theatrical precursor of the later music halls were the dance halls where legs would be exposed by 'flash dancing' and drunken girls 'ruined' by unscrupulous, lecherous boys in the back row. A notorious example was Enon Chapel built 1823 near the Strand in London, which had precipitated an earlier scandal when a corrupt Baptist minister crammed 12,000 burials under the floor, creating a 'loathsome charnel house' and possibly selling bodies for dissection. The Sunday school children complained about the 'body bugs' crawling through the floors and the foul stench. Despite worshippers regularly fainting as they breathed in noxious fumes of rotting flesh, the bodies were not discovered for many years until the minister died in 1842! After being closed in 1846 an entrepreneur converted the chapel to a low, dancing-saloon, advertising 'dancing on the dead' at threepence entry; ladies to wear stockings'. It was short-lived.

TEN POPULAR ENTERTAINERS

From the dramatic intensity of actress Ellen Terry to Agnes Beckwith, 'the most famous lady swimmer in the world', the Victorian public taste for an entertaining night out was certainly eclectic!

241

Sarah Bernhardt (1844-1923) This volatile French actress entertained and scandalised the Victorian public in equal measure. Perhaps her greatest performance was as Floria in *La Tosca* in 1887. But she gave her all in every role: when she performed the short play *Jean Marie* at a private event for Queen Victoria in Nice in 1897 the Queen later noted that [Bernhardt] 'appeared much affected herself…tears rolling down her cheeks'.

242

Jenny Lind (1820-87) The 'Swedish Nightingale' (real name Johanna Maria Lind) was a world-famous soprano with a voice of extraordinary sweetness. Jenny was in great demand as an opera singer until 1849, but she hit international stardom as a concert performer, superbly promoted by P T Barnum and inspiring 'Lind-mania' wherever she appeared. (See also Fact 67)

243

Ellen Terry (1847-1928) Queen Victoria witnessed the 8-year-old Terry's stage debut as the young prince Mamillius in *A Winter's Tale* in 1856. Despite falling on stage during this first appearance, Terry went on to become one of the most successful British actors of her generation. She toured America and Australia; career highlights include her Ophelia, Katherine of Aragon in *Henry VIII* and a terrifying Lady Macbeth.

244

Phineas Taylor Barnum (1810-91) 'Nobody ever lost a dollar underestimating the taste of the American public', observed the legendary showman and promoter PT Barnum while making a fortune from his 'travelling circus, menagerie and museum of freaks'. In 1881 he merged with business partner James Bailey to form the world-famous 'Barnum & Bailey's' three-ring circus.

245

Agnes Beckwith (born 1862) was a star attraction, known as 'the greatest lady swimmer in the world'. In 1880, she reportedly trod water for 30 hours in the 'whale tank' of the Royal Aquarium of Westminster in London.

246

Marie Lloyd (1870-1922) Marie (born Matilda Alice Victoria Wood in London) rapidly became one of the most famous of English music hall singers and comediennes. Her skill at adding lewdness to the most innocent of lyrics won her a huge following. Musical hall audiences roared with laughter, and moralists tut-tutted, as Marie sang 'a little of what you fancy does you good' accompanied by sly winks and gestures. Her funeral was attended by more than 100,000 people.

247

Harry Houdini (1874-1926) The young Houdini (European-born Erik

Opposite page **Top:** Sarah Bernhardt in 1865. **Bottom:** Ellen Terry as Lady Macbeth, by John Singer Sargent, 1889.

This page **Left:** Poster from 1895. **Right:** Dan Leno as Mrs Twankey in Aladdin at the Drury Lane Theatre, London, 1896.

Weisz, naturalised American) began his career in New York as a dime show magician, but his 'big break' came in 1899 when he concentrated on incredible acts of escapology and attracted a huge international following. He toured England and Scotland as 'The Handcuff King', before developing his most famous 'Chinese Water Torture' act, escaping from chains while suspended in a tank of water on stage.

248

Marie Taglioni (1804-84) Despite being a rather plain child with long thin arms and legs, under the tuition of her father Swedish-born Taglioni developed an ethereal quality. She became one of the world's most famous ballerinas. After her last performance in Russia in 1842, a pair of her ballet shoes was reputedly sold for 200 roubles, cooked with a sauce and eaten by a group of fans! (See also Fact 19)

249

Dan Leno (1860-1904) Leno began his career as a clog dancer, performing up to 20 times a night in northern taverns, but London audiences preferred his comic monologues and songs. By the 1880s he was the most popular music hall act in England. In 1888 he was hired as pantomime dame at the Drury Lane Theatre, and over the next 15 years, he played the dame to Marie Lloyd's principal boy (see Fact 246). At his funeral, thousands lined the streets of London.

250

Adelina Patti (1843-1919) Verdi called this supremely-talented opera star 'the finest singer that ever lived'. Born in Madrid, then moving to New York, Patti made her operatic debut in the US aged 16. By 1861 she was singing at London's Covent Garden to rapturous audiences, who thrilled to the amazing clarity of her voice. Patti demanded $5,000 in gold *before* each performance and amassed a fortune, most of which she lavished on her famous Welsh mansion, Craig-y-nos.

TEN ASPECTS OF EMPIRE

At the close of Victoria's reign, the British Empire covered more than one-fifth of the world land mass. The imperial upsurge of the later 19th century saw new territories acquired and direct controls imposed where there had been spheres of influence before.

251

The end of slavery Although the British slave trade had been abolished in 1807, and emancipation followed in 1833, slavery remained a live issue. In the American Civil War of 1861-5 many parts of Britain, especially the cotton towns of north-west England and south-west Scotland, supported the slave-owning and cotton-growing South until its defeat.

252

Emigration The 19th century saw a great outward flow of British people, as new 'white' territories opened up in Canada, the US, Australia and New Zealand. These colonies offered new economic incentives and administrative job opportunities.

253

The 'informal' empire The cast-iron railways and cattle market in Montevideo, Uruguay, are branded 'Made in Birmingham'. Although Britain had almost no colonies in South America, British economic and political influence there was immense.

254

The Indian Mutiny and the end of the East India Company Established in 1612, the joint stock East India Company had grown ever greater in power and economic command in India. By the mid-19th century it controlled most of the sub-continent. Bloody rebellion broke out in 1857, which was put down by July 1858 with great bloodshed on both sides, and direct rule by the Crown was established the next month. (See also Fact 204)

255

Empress of India It galled Queen Victoria that her daughter Vicky, wife of the Kaiser, was an empress; as a mere queen, she lacked precedence among European royalty. Benjamin Disraeli, her favourite Prime Minister, took the matter in hand, and Victoria was created Empress of India on 1 May 1876.

256

The Scramble for Africa In the final quarter of the 19th century, the European powers divided much of sub-Saharan Africa between them. The British had regarded the 'dark continent' as principally their own enclave and colonisation had been slow; as the French, Belgians and

"NEW CROWNS FOR OLD ONES!"

Opposite page **Left:** An emigrating couple in *The Last of England* by Ford Madox Brown. **Top right:** 'British Vengeance': a 'British' lion attacks a murderous 'Indian' tiger in this cartoon printed after the Sepoy mutiny of 1857. **Bottom right:** Prime Minister Disraeli hands a pleased 'Empress' Victoria the crown of India, drawn by John Tenniel, 1876.

This page **Left:** A 1951 cover of Kipling's ever-popular *Just So Stories.* **Right:** *General Gordon's Last Stand,* depicting events at Khartoum in 1885, by George William Joy.

Germans began to acquire territories and influence, relationships became increasingly antagonistic. Congresses in Berlin (1878) and Brussels (1890) defused the tensions and sanctioned division of territories.

257

By Jingo! Jingoism was the imperialistic chauvinism typical of the later 19th century. It had its origins in the popular support for Disraeli's policy to send a fleet to check the Russians in 1878, captured in the music hall song: 'We don't want to fight/ But, by Jingo if we do/ We've got the ships, we've got the men/ We've got the money too!'

258

Rudyard Kipling The novelist, poet and short story writer Rudyard Kipling (1865-1936) embodied the spirit of the British in India. Born in Bombay, he established an early reputation as a journalist before coming to England in 1889. Many of his books and stories for children remain popular: *The Jungle Book* (1894), *Kim* (1901) and the *Just So Stories* (1902).

259

Australian federation Established as a penal colony in New South Wales, the colonies in Australia were formed by division from the original settlement or by exploration and settlement. Extensive land grants, sheep rearing and the discovery of gold opened up the continent. The colonies gained independence from British rule in 1850, followed by Western Australia in 1890. The Australian Commonwealth Act 1900, created a parliament in a new capital, Canberra.

260

Gordon and Khartoum A military hero in the Crimea and China, Charles Gordon was the enlightened administrator of the Sudan on behalf of Egypt, 1874-80. Recalled in 1884 to quell the revolt of the messianic Mahdi, Gordon died in Khartoum after a 10-month siege. His death unleashed public anger in Britain against Gladstone for not sending a relief force, and he became a popular hero of Empire.

Left to right: The murderous Dowager Cixi (T'zu-hsi) Empress; Queen Liliuokalani of Hawaii, pictured in 1887; Eugénie, Empress of the French, in a print after the painting by Franz Xaver Winterhalter, *c*1850.

261

Empress Cixi (T'zu-hsi) of China (1835-1908) The Dragon Empress began as a humble Imperial concubine in the Forbidden City, then poisoned her way to power and continued her murderous rule to maintain absolute control over China. Hated and feared, one of her last acts as she lay dying was to murder her own nephew and install a child in his place, Pu-Yi, who was to be China's last emperor.

262

Queen Liliuokalani of Hawaii (1838-1917) The Polynesian Kingdom of Hawaii had to fight off predatory American interests, which wished to annexe her kingdom. Liliuokalani succeeded when the male line failed, and attended Queen Victoria's Golden Jubilee.

TEN OTHER VICTORIAN 'QUEENS'

Victoria had many female contemporaries across the globe. The power behind a weak king was often an interesting, more intelligent woman.

263

Empress Elizabeth of Austria (1837-98) 'Sissy' was the unconventional wife of the staid Emperor Franz Josef, adored by her husband, yet trapped in an unhappy, arranged marriage which produced the tragic Crown Prince Rudolph, who was to commit suicide with his mistress at Mayerling in 1889. After years wandering around Europe to avoid the stifling Viennese court, Sissy was stabbed to death by an anarchist on Lake Geneva.

264

Queen Wilhelmina of the Netherlands (1880-1962) Queen Victoria thought the young Wilhelmina who acceded in 1890 'cute' and said, 'she knows how to behave with charming manners'. Wilhelmina's stoic resistance during the Second World War was an inspiration to her people.

265

Queen Isabella II of Spain (1830-1904) Queen Isabella, whose portly frame gave her a passing resemblance to Queen Victoria, sat uneasily on the throne of Spain, opposed by male chauvinists. Her reign was a catalogue of intrigues, ending in a revolution and her departure in 1868.

266

Queen Ranavalona III of Madagascar (1861-1917) Three women of that name ruled 19th-century Madagascar, but it was the third who distinguished herself by trying to resist French and British attempts to annex her kingdom. Ultimately, the French won, exiling her to Algiers.

267

Masalanabo Modjadji II, the Rain Queen (d1894) The Modjadji or Rain Queen, invested with mythical weather-controlling properties was a tribal ruler in northern South Africa, who probably inspired H Rider Haggard's *She*. When captured by the Boer general Piet Joubert, instead of a great queen resplendent in jewels, from her tent 'an old wrinkled black woman was carried out on a litter', to the disappointment of all present.

268

Sultan Shahjahan Begum of Bhopal (1838-1901) The Begum came from a line of strong female rulers in a fairly unconventional Muslim dynasty. Her mother had supported the British during the Mutiny of 1857, and her daughter followed in her footsteps, being progressive in founding schools, colleges and mosques.

269

Empress Carlota of Mexico (1840-1927) The young Charlotte of Saxe-Coburg was a cousin of Queen Victoria. She accompanied her husband Maximilian in their romantic but ill-fated bid for the crown of Mexico, but the Emperor was deposed and died bravely in front of a firing squad. Carlota suffered a nervous breakdown and lived the rest of her life as a recluse.

270

Empress Eugénie of the French (1826-1920) Fashionable Eugénie was stunning in comparison to Victoria's dumpy dowdiness. An unexpected but warm relationship developed between the women and when Eugénie was forced into exile with her husband, Napoleon III in 1871 it was in England that they found refuge. 'My legend' she said 'has taken shape: at the beginning of the reign, I was the frivolous woman only interested in clothes; towards the end of the Empire, I became the *femme fatale*, responsible for everything that went wrong! And legends always get the upper hand of history'.

TEN SOCIAL MILESTONES

Reform was one of the main characteristics of Victorian Britain. Old institutions were swept away, or were overwhelmed by the swelling population and the growth of the economy. But the benefits were uneven; as many suffered as prospered.

271

Penny Post The brainchild of Rowland Hill (1795-1879), the Penny Post was inaugurated on 1 May 1840 (See Penny Black, page 73). Communication came within everyone's grasp. A fast, efficient service spawned innovations that we take for granted, including post boxes, post cards, adhesive stamps, and envelopes.

272

The Chartists' apogee Chartism was the greatest grassroots organisation of the Victorian age. The Great Charter, dating from 1838, called for social justice, electoral reform and the vote for all men. Over 5 million signed, and many turned out to demonstrate on 10 April 1838.

273

Social investigation To collect and measure was, it seemed to the Victorians, to understand. Among the enduring legacies of this belief are the works of social investigators who documented life, labour and poverty, among them Henry Mayhew and Charles Booth who exposed the makeshift housing and the extent of poverty in areas of London. Seebohm Rowntree (from the famous chocolate family) in York in 1897 conducted one of the first scientific studies of nutrition and poverty. (See this book's endpapers for poverty maps)

274

Contagious Diseases Acts 1864-9 Legislation designed to combat the spread of venereal disease in garrison and port towns – and so stop the degradation of enlisted men – required the registration and forced physical examination of 'common prostitutes'. Vigorous opposition to the acts and their double standard – men's sexual activity was not curbed – was led by the active social purity campaigner Josephine Butler and the Ladies' National Association. Repeal came in 1886.

275

Reform Acts 1867 and 1884 Gradually, following the great 1832 Reform Act, the franchise was to be extended to all men, and eventually women. In 1867 urban skilled workers were given the vote, but still only a third of adult males were eligible. In 1887 this increased to 60 per cent, with the franchise property qualifications extended to the countryside. Only in 1918 were all men over 21 given the vote; it came to all women over 21 in 1928.

276

Married Women's Property Acts 1870, 1882 Milestones in the progressive improvement in the legal status of women, the acts overturned the principle that married women were the possessions of their husband, and gave them rights over property.

WIGAN ELECTION.

A PUBLIC

MEETING

WILL BE HELD ON

THURSDAY, JAN. 6th, 1881,

IN THE

PUBLIC HALL, KING STREET,

TO PROMOTE THE UNCONDITIONAL REPEAL

OF THE

CONTAGIOUS DISEASES ACTS

RELATING TO WOMEN.

CHAIR TO BE TAKEN AT 8 O'CLOCK.

THE MEETING WILL BE ADDRESSED BY

J. BIRBECK NEVINS, Esq. M.D.

OF LIVERPOOL;

T. CARSON, Esq., M.R.C.S.I.

OF LIVERPOOL;

WILLIAM T. SWAN, Esq.

OF LONDON, REPRESENTATIVE OF THE NORTHERN COUNTIES LEAGUE FOR THE ABOLITION OF STATE REGULATION OF VICE.

EDMUND JONES,

PRESIDENT OF THE NATIONAL WORKMEN'S LEAGUE FOR REPEAL OF THE CONTAGIOUS DISEASES ACTS.

ELECTORS! No question upon which either Mr. LANCASTER or Mr. POWELL will have to record his Vote, if returned to Parliament, is of greater importance than whether the one-sided, unjust, and unconstitutional CONTAGIOUS DISEASES ACTS, 1866-9, should continne to disgrace our Statute Book, or be unconditionally repealed.

Every Voter, Liberal or Conservative, is earnestly invited.

WALL, PRINTER, WALLGATE, WIGAN.

Left to right: Painted from sketches made in the Westminster workhouse in London, Sir Hubert von Herkomer's *Eventide: A Scene in The Westminster Union* (1878) is thought to be the only Victorian genre painting of a workhouse; Educating the poor in *The Ragged School*, one half of a coloured stereoscopic photograph by James Elliot, *c*1860; Wigan election poster for a public meeting to debate issues from the social purity campaign, 1881.

277

Education Act 1870 One of the most enduring achievements of Gladstone's great reforming administration of 1868-74 was the establishment of the principle of elementary education for all.

278

Public Health Acts 1872, 1875 As urban populations continued to grow massively, so pressure on public health grew in parallel. A control system of sorts was created in 1848, and the end of cholera by 1866 resulted from recognising the effects of foul water supplies. (See also Fact 376)

279

1883 FA Cup Final Originally a middle-class, strictly amateur game, standard rules for football were drawn up under the new Football Association in 1863, and the game's social reach widened. The Old Etonians lost in 1883, and the game changed forever. (See also Fact 362)

280

The Maiden Tribute of Modern Babylon The campaigning journalist W T Stead exposed the sex trade and child prostitution under this sensationalist title in his *Pall Mall Gazette* in 1885. His efforts brought fame and imprisonment for him, and the passage of the Criminal Law Amendment Act raising the female age of consent to 16. A late amendment criminalising male homosexual activity was only repealed in 1967.

TEN POPULAR SEASIDE RESORTS

The song 'You can do a lot of things at the seaside you can't do in town' *reflected a feeling that many Victorians shared at Britain's seaside resorts. Workers, eager for time off (enforced by the Bank Holiday Act in 1871), flocked to the coast on the new railways.*

281

Scarborough Already a fashionable spa town, Scarborough changed dramatically in the 19th century with the influx of large numbers of tourists. Sir Joseph Paxton, who had designed the Crystal Palace for the Great Exhibition, redesigned the spa buildings, which soon attracted top music hall stars.

282

Brighton received the royal seal of approval when the flamboyant Prince Regent, the future King George IV, built his famous oriental-style pavilion. Queen Victoria found the fashionable town wanting in privacy and the pavilion unsuitable for her growing family's needs. The building and grounds were sold to the town in 1850.

283

Llandudno The Welsh seaside town was one of comparatively few British resorts that permitted mixed bathing, a habit which many people still considered to be outrageous in 1900!

Opposite page **Top left:** Scarborough, the Spa Promenade, 1890. **Top right:** On Yarmouth Sands, seaside fun by Paul Martin, 1892. **Bottom:** Blackpool, the South Jetty by Francis Frith, 1890. This page **Top:** Mr Punch with Toby the dog and a clown, *c*1850. **Bottom:** A song sheet illustrated by Walter Crane, 1883.

284

Blackpool Competition between the new resorts spurred local businessmen to build novelty attractions for the burgeoning tourist market. Blackpool's promenade, Winter Gardens and, by 1879 electric lights, fascinated visitors. The famous Blackpool Tower opened in 1894.

285

Southport Accessible by rail from 1848, Southport became known as a more elegant alternative to Blackpool and attracted Lancashire mill workers and their families. The town's pleasure pier, opened in 1860 with refreshment rooms and a tram, was the second longest in Britain.

286

Ramsgate The upmarket Kent resort was evoked in a 19th-century ladies' journal: 'When the sun is bright and the air warm…and the rows of white and party-coloured bathing machines…and the many-hued parasols of the loungers glance in the sunlight, then Ramsgate… is a pleasant and animated scene'.

287

Bridlington Some towns passed special legislation to prevent the drunkenness and disruptive behaviour that long-term residents blamed on day trippers. In 1889, Bridlington passed an act that enabled any resident to demand a street musician leave their neighbourhood or pay a 40-shilling fine.

288

Margate Marked class differences began to distinguish one town from another as the number of seaside resorts rapidly increased. In 1856, the *Illustrated Times* remarked, 'Margate is what is termed vulgar, that is to say, it does not wear gloves, never dresses before dinner, and likes hot rum-and-water with lemon in it. It is Ramsgate smoking a clay pipe, with its coat and boots off.'

289

Yarmouth Photographer Paul Martin recorded seaside resort visitors' free and easy behaviour on the beach at Yarmouth using a 'detective' camera that he disguised in a leather box. His 1890s images of couples frolicking on the sand, beach entertainments and scantily-clad swimmers testify that the Victorians were not as prudish as people now often claim.

290

Ventnor This town on Queen Victoria's beloved Isle of Wight became extremely popular as a seaside resort after being mentioned in the Queen's doctor Sir James Clark's *The Influence of Climate in the Prevention and Cure of Chronic Diseases* (1830). In 1895, one travel writer noted, 'Ventnor is essentially a place that has been made by doctors, and nothing can be more astonishing than the rapidity with which the tiny fishing hamlet has been transformed into a fashionable resort.'

TEN WEIRD VICTORIAN FASHIONS

Technological advances and improvements in living standards ensured that more people could afford decorative and fashionable clothing and indulge in all the ingenuity, excess and engineering wizardry that 19th-century fashion had to offer.

291

Crinolines First appearing in 1856 as a welcome alternative to heavy layers of petticoats, the crinoline was a lightweight metal cage that allowed the skirts of Victorian dresses to reach fantastic proportions. It was a piece of underwear engineering mercilessly lampooned by satirists who suggested that such structures were responsible for countless social faux pas, indelicacies and accidents.

292

The corset This iconic undergarment, which shaped the upper torso and nipped in the waist to extreme slimness, invoked some of the most contradictory opinions about 19th-century dress. The corset created outward elegance combined with inner agony, as women suffered lack of breath and, occasionally, crushed internal organs. 'But better that', said tight-laced ladies through gritted teeth, 'than be thought a "loose" woman'!

293

Purple haze The invention of mauve aniline dye by the young chemist William Perkin in 1856 was greeted with great excitement. However, its over-enthusiastic use as a fabric dye in England led the French commentator Hippolyte Taine to bemoan, 'there is something peculiar in the condition of the English retina'.

294

False hair In the early 1870s it was fashionable for women to pile their heads with pounds of false locks, the best quality being human hair. Such was the demand for chignons, switches and bandeaux that salacious newspaper reports of hair being obtained from tuberculosis sufferers or mortuary corpses caused real alarm.

295

Mutton chops Extravagant facial hair was a must (for men!). Among the most striking styles were mutton chops. The hair extended from the ear over each cheek in a distinctive chop-like shape.

Left to right: This bystander cops an eyeful on a windy day as a lady 'takes off' in her crinoline, 1859; *A correct view of the new machine for winding up ladies* c1830, one of many anti-fashion etchings published by Thomas McLean; Poet Matthew Arnold with a splendid pair of mutton chop whiskers, c1870s; Cruikshank's *Exhibition of Bloomers in Hyde Park*, a satirical illustration from 1852; Victorian bathers at Blackpool, 1895.

296

Bloomers Named after an American Mrs Bloomer and inspired by the dress of Turkish women, these voluminous trousers were introduced into Britain in the 1850s. Intended as a practical form of dress, to be worn beneath a knee-length crinoline skirt, they were greeted with scorn and derision. 'Bloomerism' faded after six months.

297

Aesthetic dress In an attempt to resist the tightly-laced, mid 19th-century fashionable ideal of womanly beauty, fans of artistic dress draped themselves in fluid, floating material in muted colours. Again, aesthetic dress attracted ridicule, especially because of the exclusive, cliquey nature of its advocates.

298

Knickerbockers While women suffered in corsets and crinolines, these loose fitting breeches, gathered at the knee, were worn by Victorian boys and sportsmen, who both required freedom of movement. Oscar Wilde was a fan, championing knickerbockers as an alternative to stuffy, uncomfortable masculine attire.

299

Digit socks This woollen stocking, which encased each toe in its own sheath to reduce perspiration and aid circulation, was a striking element of the new Sanitary Woollen System, promoted in 1884 by Dr Jaeger. He sought to convince the Victorian public that wool was the healthiest fibre to be used for clothing, bedding and other textiles.

300

Beachwear Visiting the seaside for pleasure and sea bathing became increasingly popular in the 19th century, but the wearing of figure-hugging lycra was still a century or more away. Mixed bathing resorts were rare before 1900, and bathing huts were still drawn down to the water's edge on women-only beaches. Womens' costumes were neck-to-knee garments made from sagging wool.

TEN VICTORIAN ARTISTS

Art in Britain during Victoria's reign took its own direction, striving for artistic and sometimes social realism, while largely ignoring seismic developments on the continent. With Albert's guidance, Victoria became a great patron of more traditional art, with a preference for foreign artists such as Winterhalter and Angeli.

301

Joseph Mallord William Turner (1775-1851) Although his life spanned the reigns of four monarchs from George III, Turner must be the most revolutionary and influential artist to have lived in Queen Victoria's time. However, she firmly resisted the appeal of his later paintings, when he created some of his most celebrated and radical works.

302

John Martin (1789-1854) No list of Victorian painters would be complete without at least one mystic or visionary artist. Martin's panoramic scenes, crammed with minute figures in anticipation of De Mille's Hollywood epics, appealed to both Victoria and Albert, who bought one of Martin's most famous works, *The Eve of the Deluge*, in 1841.

303

Paul Delaroche (1797-1856) This foreign artist was an Anglophile from post-revolutionary France who came to England when Victoria was still a child and created some of the most memorable images from British history. This was a period when Anglomania gripped many French artists of all kinds. Delaroche's acutely portrayed scenes helped inspire a

new generation of English artists to evoke their own country's past *(above).*

304

Sir Edwin Landseer (1802-73) A flawed genius and Victoria's favourite artist, whom she thought the cleverest artist there was. He could paint anything brilliantly but became famous for his sentimental portraits of animals which the Victorians lapped up. Though no sculptor himself, in 1857 he agreed to design the bronze lions in Trafalgar Square. His early studies of such wild beasts had taken place in the old Menagerie at the Tower of London.

305

Franz Xaver Winterhalter (1805-73) This international portrait painter from the Black Forest arrived in Britain not long after Victoria and Albert's marriage and he rapidly became their favourite portrait painter. His suave, sentimental works soon created the ideal image of the Victorian family epitomised by Victoria and Albert. Winterhalter returned to Britain several times to paint the royal couple and their growing family, and created at least 120 royal portraits.

306

Carlo, Baron Marochetti (1805-67) Marochetti was a very talented Italian-born and French-trained sculptor who was a nobleman by birth. He went straight into Victoria and Albert's list of favourite artists in spite of some nationalistic opposition to his success with commissions for public art. Although no longer a familiar name, his public works include some of London's landmarks such as Richard I on horseback outside the Houses of Parliament and Robert Stephenson (of 'Rocket' fame) at Euston Station.

307

William Powell Frith (1819-1909) Frith became a highly popular observer of everyday life in all its myriad detail, and is perhaps the epitome of a Victorian painter. His detailed paintings of 'modern life', including subjects such as the new railway terminals and bathing resorts, are full of social observation yet not too overtly political to deter a royal patron like Victoria!

308

John Ruskin (1819-1900) Hugely influential as an artist, also as art patron,

Previous page **Left:** *The Eve of the Deluge*, John Martin, 1840. **Right:** *The Execution of Lady Jane Grey*, Paul Delaroche, 1833.

This page **Left:** *Monarch of the Glen*, by Sir Edwin Landseer, 1851. **Right:** *Mariana*, by Sir John Everett Millais, 1851.

writer and philanthropist, Ruskin was the first Slade Professor of Art at Oxford. You might not hang one of his watercolours in your all-time gallery of art but there is no doubting his huge impact on British art: as a visionary socialist thinker, critic, talent-scout, famously-jilted husband (to another artist here, Millais) and champion of 'modern art' who was at odds with many of his contemporaries.

309

Sir John Everett Millais (1829-96) While Turner created a revolution in painting that had repercussions around the world, another storm in Victorian art was stirred up by a group of wild young artists who wanted to turn the cultural clock back – the Pre-Raphaelites. Millais was remarkable in the way he moved from iconoclast to Royal Academy President.

310

Sir Alfred Gilbert (1854-1934) One of the few truly modern artists to emerge in late Victorian England when the country's art world was considered rather backward compared to their continental rivals. He made one of our most famous sculptures – 'Eros' in Piccadilly Circus – who is in fact Anteros, the Greek god of philanthropic love. (See also Fact 311)

TEN POSITIVE ASPECTS OF THE ERA

Not all aspects of the Victorian period are admirable, but these represent 19th-century virtues, including an enlightened responsibility among some wealthy people and a swelling of civic pride as towns and cities grew larger and more complex.

311

Charity and philanthropy For some, great wealth came with a social conscience. Some say that the statue of Eros in London's Piccadilly is not even Anteros (see Fact 310) but the Angel of Christian Charity. The statue was erected to commemorate Lord Shaftesbury, one of the greatest philanthropists of his age. Eros is a testament to the generosity of the Victorian heart.

312

Municipal parks The municipal park, an amenity that we all take for granted in our towns and cities, grew from a sense of civic pride and a belief that people should have a right to recreation, an appreciation of nature and an opportunity to improve their lot in life.

313

Public buildings Town hall, prison, school, museum and art gallery, hospital, swimming pool, public lavatory – except for prisons we might all have visited them at one time or another, and they are integral to the social fabric. Yet few existed before the Victorian era and the public gathering that most engender is a symbol of the Victorian zeal for organisation and social cohesion.

314

Urbanisation In 1851, the results of the census showed that Great Britain had become the first nation in human history where more people lived in towns and cities than in the country. This is a trend that has enveloped the world and is a defining characteristic of our civilisation.

315

Communication At the beginning of the reign, communication was slow; messages could take six weeks or longer to reach remote areas of the globe. By 1901 much of the world was linked by telegraph, defined by Queen Victoria's

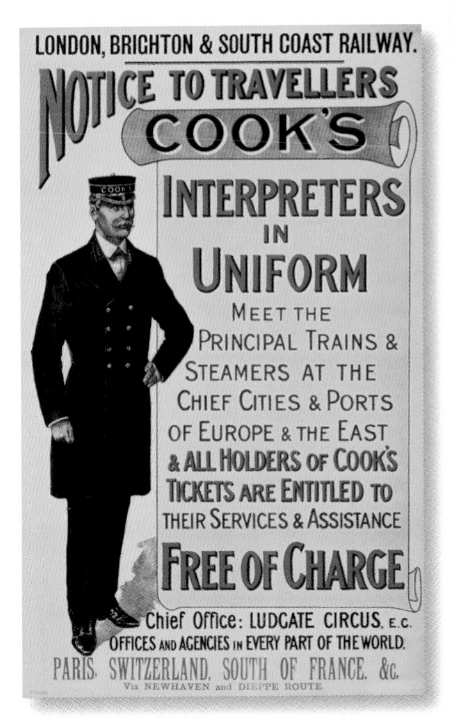

Opposite page **Top:** *Piccadilly Circus at Night* by Earnest Dudley Heath, *c*1893. **Bottom:** A public park, Union Terrace Gardens in Aberdeen, *c*1900. This page **Far left:** Thomas Cook poster advertising free interpreters for package deal travellers. **Left:** Legendary cricketer W G Grace, caricatured by Alfred Gish Bryan, *c*1874. **Right:** Alexander Graham Bell (1847-1922) *c*1876. **Bottom:** The spectacular arches of London's Paddington Station, built by I K Brunel, in *The Railway Station* (detail) by William Powell Frith, 1862.

message to her global empire, at the press of a button. Alexander Graham Bell's 'electrical speech machine', was invented in 1876 and first used by the Queen at Osborne in 1878. Now over half the world's population have a mobile phone.

316

Great works of engineering The Victorian achievements in great feats of engineering are legendary, from the network of railways to thousands of miles of sewers, great bridges and tunnels, but underlying it was boundless self-confidence and a sense that nothing was impossible. (See also pages 74-7)

317

Globalisation We think of globalisation as a relatively recent innovation, but the Victorian age was a technological one, and the British Empire the first truly global phenomenon. The tendrils of British influence went far beyond those parts of the map coloured red, while English gradually supplanted all other languages as the universal means of communication. (See also pages 86-7)

318

The package tour holiday Tourism was an 18th-century invention, but confined to the rich. In the 1840s, Thomas Cook began organising short excursions, negotiating reduced ticket prices with the railway companies for rallies and short breaks and thereby bringing prices within the reach of more modest incomes.

319

Organised sport Cricket, football, rugby, the Olympic Games: these and many other sports are the obsessions of our own age. With their usual efficiency and flair for organising, the Victorians codified rules and set up organisations, thus allowing traditional sports to spread around the world.

320

Births, Marriages, Deaths The increasing maturity of British society led the state to take an increasingly direct role in the organisation of people's lives. One of the first acts of Victoria's reign in 1837 was Civil Registration, requiring everyone to record births, marriages and deaths at the local registry office. We now find these records indispensable for geneaological research.

TEN PLEASURES AND PASTIMES

More people could afford leisure pursuits, as disposable incomes grew. For all the anguish and deprivation that people experienced, we also know that the Victorians could enjoy themselves.

321

Photography Various inventions in Britain and France in the 1830s gave birth to photography, offering everyone an opportunity to see themselves – and cheaply. In 1851 there were 51 photographers listed in the census; ten years later there were 2,534. Queen Victoria herself was one of the first to recognise photography's social value, enduring the long exposures needed in the medium's early days.

322

Household Words Many of Charles Dickens's (1812-70) multi-layered fictions, from the light-hearted *Pickwick Papers* (1837) to *Great Expectations* (1860), first appeared in serial publications. The greatest of them was his own weekly journal *Household Words*, published from 1850; readers waited impatiently for the next instalment of news of *David Copperfield* or *Little Dorrit.*

323

Parlour songs Did Victorians really cover up piano legs out of prudishness? No, that's a myth. Did they gather round the piano to sing songs at home? They did. Pianos were mass-produced (twice as many were made in 1890 as in 1850); publishers of sheet music could barely keep up with demand. 'What is a home without a piano?' was an advertisement spotted by the social investigator Charles Booth in London's impoverished East End.

324

Music hall Providing mass working class entertainment in London and the large industrial towns, music halls developed from music and acrobatics in pleasure gardens and pub sing-songs into specialist concert halls. The first date from the 1830s; by 1875 there were more than 300 in London alone.

Opposite page **Top:** 'Photography on the Common' from the photographic collection *Street Life of London*, 1877, by John Thomson. **Bottom:** A Victorian family sing-song. This page **Far left:** Programme from the Oxford Theatre, a popular music hall in London's West End, opened 1861. **Below left:** Performers in Gilbert and Sullivan's comic opera *The Mikado*, 1885. **Left:** Commemorative medal showing the Lumière brothers. **Below right:** Society ladies cycling in Hyde Park, 1896, from *Vanity Fair*.

325

The birth of cinema The Lumière brothers brought the newly-invented moving pictures from Paris to London in 1896. A new medium was born, that would define the 20th century and eclipse many Victorian entertainments. Queen Victoria's Diamond Jubilee was one of the first events to be filmed.

326

The Savoy operas W S Gilbert and Sir Arthur Sullivan devised some of the most successful musical productions of the Victorian age, the comic Savoy operas. *Trial by Jury* (1875) was their first success; the partnership ended in 1896.

327

The seaside Brighton, Margate and Scarborough can claim to have invented the seaside, as holiday destinations in the 1820s and 1830s. Piers, beach fun, donkey rides and minstrels were soon enjoyed in resorts around the coast. (See also pages 92-3)

328

Days out – Chestnut Sunday One of Queen Victoria's early acts, in 1838, was to open Hampton Court Palace to the public, and the weekend stately home visit was born. The greatest of all the days out was 'Chestnut Sunday' in spring at Hampton Court when 'cockneys' descended in droves to picnic and frolic.

329

Oh, Sir Jasper! Sensation, dastardly villains and improbable coincidences marked the plots of the most common theatrical entertainment. They developed from romances with musical interludes into emotional heart-wringing dramas with happy endings, such as *Lady Audley's Secret* (1863) or *The Ticket-of-leave Man* (1863).

330

Bicycling Although bicycles had been around from the 1860s onwards, the twin inventions of the safety bicycle and pneumatic tyres made the 1890s into the golden age of cycling.

TEN HEALTH AND BEAUTY 'TIPS'

Queen Victoria lived in a world where women were supposed to be naturally beautiful – and yet ever-increasing numbers of drugs, potions and tricks were available for the image-conscious.

331

Slimming aids The rotund Queen in later life was not a great advert for the slimming aid 'Benger's Food', probably because she mistakenly consumed it in addition, instead of as an alternative to, her usual diet.

332

Hair dye Victorian values were set firmly against make-up and artifice to improve the appearance. A book called *Good Society,* published in 1869 by a 'countess' recommended that women should never 'change the colour of the hair by means of fashionable dyes…practices of this kind are simply and strictly immodest'.

333

Lipstick was thought equally horrendous: 'There is no man who does not shrink back with disgust from the idea of kissing a pair of painted lips.'

334

The natural look Despite public disapproval, Victorian women clearly did employ cosmetics – they just tried to be discreet. 'A sweet and modest woman should be careful to an extreme degree in using artificial expedients during the daytime', they were advised, 'as the manifestly made-up woman is too atrocious a blot on the landscape to even discuss'. However 'at night…the artificial light makes it possible for a woman literally to put on her war paint'.

335

Beauty secrets Madame Rachel was a notorious charlatan who, at the height of her career, charged 20 guineas for 'enamelling', making over a lady's face. She demanded a fortune to reveal her 'Secret of Eternal Youth' (so-called 'Magnetic Rock Dew Water of Sahara'). She ended up on trial in 1868 and again in 1878, and died in prison.

336

Pain relief Victoria was the first member of the royal family to use chloroform – 'that blessed chloroform…soothing and delightful beyond measure', as she called it – to ease the pains of her eighth labour in 1853. This did much to make the treatment respectable in the face of moral disapproval. 'In no case could it be justifiable', claimed *The Lancet,* 'to administer chloroform in perfectly ordinary labour'. The Queen thought otherwise.

337

Keeping regular The Victorians were terrified of constipation. Queen Victoria tried to avoid it by drinking large glasses of water and taking a weekly purge.

338

Bathing beauties By the end of Victoria's reign, plumbed-in baths and showers in dedicated bathrooms were becoming more common, and daily bathing was starting to be considered essential in polite society.

Left to right: Advertisements for Benger's Food and beauty aid Beetham's Glycerine and Cucumber for 'soft, white skin'; Luxury! A bathroom shower, 1900; 'For an elegant figure and good health,' two battery-powered beauties show off their Harness' Electric Corsets.

339

Shock treatment Being treated with electricity was very much in vogue. Patented machines gave patients small shocks intended to help them lose weight, calm nerves, or remove tiredness, while all sorts of dubious claims were made for 'electric corsets'!

340

Royal pick-me-up In old age, Victoria suffered from various aches and pains, a bad back, sleeplessness, indigestion, and failing eyesight. After a bad night, her doctor recommended that she get through her waking hours with the aid of 'a little milk and whisky several times a day'. She also treated herself with large doses of the popular sedative chloral.

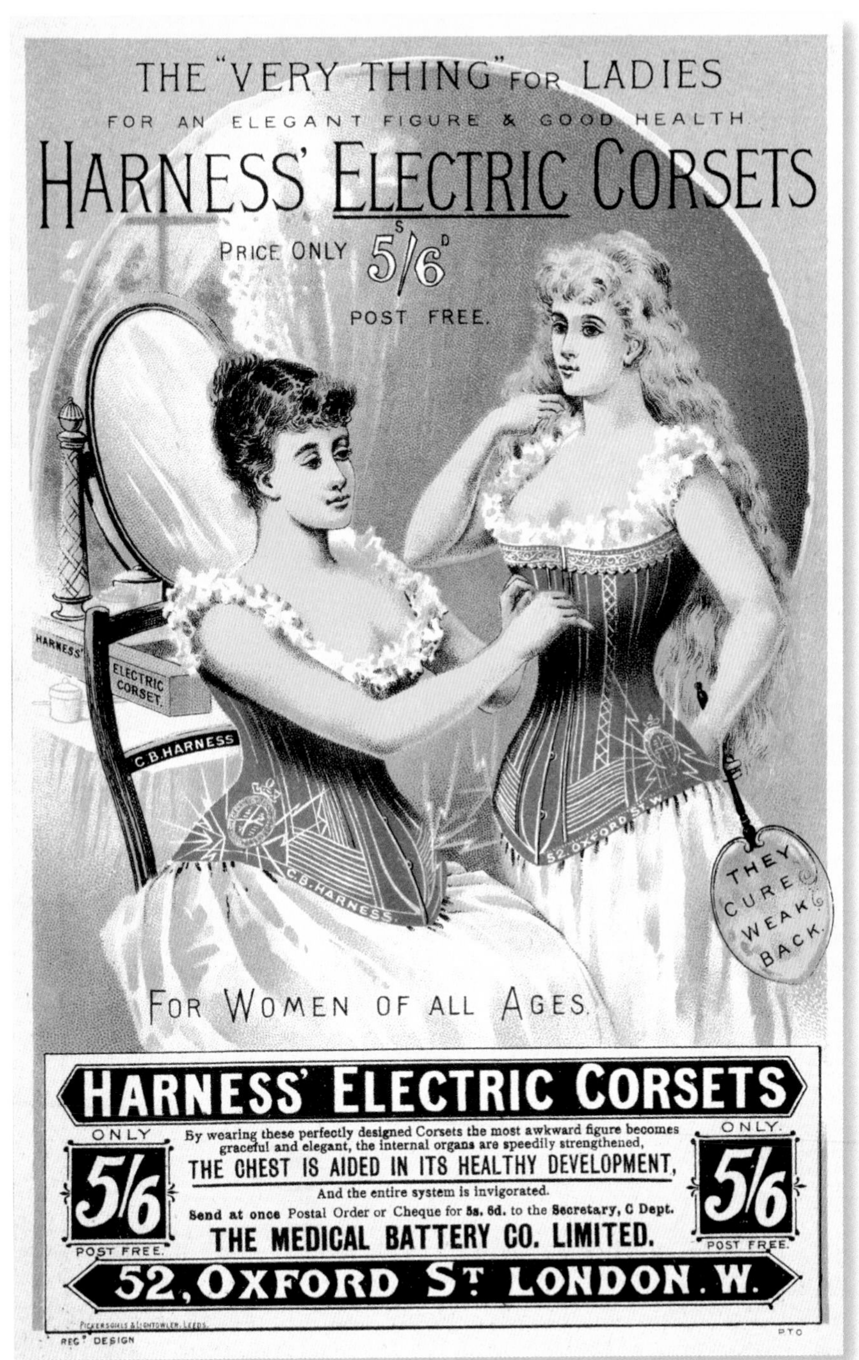

TEN TYPES OF HOUSEHOLD SERVANT

During Queen Victoria's reign there were more domestic servants than at any other point in history, and the majority of them were women. The number of servants employed by a single family ranged from over a hundred in a great house, down to a single maid in a lower middle-class home.

341

The senior male servant was **the butler,** who was responsible for the hiring and firing of the footmen and other indoor male staff. He was in charge of the dining areas, cellars and pantries (where china and silverware were kept) and his duties included arranging the dinner table, announcing dinner, carving joints of meat and serving wine.

342

The senior female servant was **the housekeeper,** who was always called 'Mrs' by the other servants, regardless of whether she was married or not. She was responsible for running the household and for keeping the household accounts. She hired and fired all the female staff, with the exception of the lady's maid. (See Fact 344)

343

The valet worked directly with the master of the house, taking care of his wardrobe, helping him dress and undress, making travel arrangements and dealing with expenses. Professional cook and bestselling author Mrs Beeton described the valet's role in the morning: 'Having thus seen his master dressed, if he is about to go out, the valet will hand

Left to right: A butler waits on an unhappy couple in *The Marriage of Convenience,* by Sir William Quiller Orchardson, 1883; *The Servants' Magazine* was the best place to advertise for new staff; This saucy maid takes an order on the household internal 'telephone'.

him his cane, gloves, and hat, the latter well brushed on the outside with a soft brush, and wiped inside with a clean handkerchief, respectfully attend him to the door, and open it for him, and receive his last orders for the day'.

344

The lady's maid, found only in the homes of the wealthy, was in constant attendance on the lady of the house and would help her dress and undress, do her hair and make and repair clothes. She was expected to be literate, neat, and have excellent needlework skills and, as she was always seen with her mistress, her clothes were much better than those of the other female servants. She was often regarded with suspicion by her colleagues.

THE
SERVANTS' MAGAZINE.
No. 13. New Series.] 1 January, 1868. [Price One Penny.

345

Footmen answered the door, delivered letters, set up the table (under the butler's supervision), waited at dinner, polished the silver, and accompanied the family carriage on outings. They were often the most visible servants in the house so were chosen for their good looks. In the best households they were perfectly matched in height and trained to act in unison, knocking on doors or serving dishes with a synchronised flourish.

346

The housemaid was a general maid around the house and, depending on the number of servants kept by the family, could fulfil many different roles such as chamber maid, parlour maid, between maid, kitchen maid or laundry maid.

347

Laundry maids were employed by the wealthiest families to wash, dry and iron all their laundry. In the days before washing machines, this was a major task and the quantity of items to be cleaned could be enormous. Water was brought from an outside pump and heated over the kitchen fire in a large tub. Clothes were pounded with a 'dolly peg' (a long wooden utensil with a handle) or scrubbed on a washboard. A mangle was used to squeeze out excess water and the clothes were then hung to dry. Flat irons, heated up on a range, or stove, were common and when one was being used, another was heating up. Electric irons were introduced in the 1880s but were expensive and dangerous to use as they were not earthed.

348

The maid-of-all-work, or general servant, was the most common of all. Employed by lower middle-class families, they were often young teenage girls and were responsible for all the household chores. Hannah Cullwick (1833-1909), a maid-of-all-work for a Kilburn upholsterer, kept a diary that illustrates a typical day, which could last from 6.00am until 11.00pm. This is just part of her day: 'swept and dusted the rooms and the hall, laid the cloth and got breakfast up - cleaned two pairs of boots - made the beds and emptied the slops, cleared and washed the breakfast things up - cleaned the plate - cleaned the knives and got dinner up - cleared away, cleaned the kitchen up - unpacked a hamper - took two chickens to Mrs Brewer's and brought a message back - made a tart and picked and gutted two ducks and roasted them - cleaned the steps and flags on my knees, blackleaded the scraper in the front of the house - cleaned the street flags too on my knees - had tea - cleared away - washed up in the scullery - cleaned the pantry on my knees and scoured the tables - scrubbed the flags round the house and cleaned the window sills...'

349

Between maids, or 'tweenies' as they were known, worked partly as housemaids and partly as kitchenmaids in smaller households. They sat at the bottom of the servants' hierarchy, along with the scullery maids, and were often badly treated by the more senior servants.

350

Scullery maids were the lowest ranking and often the youngest of the female servants. Working hours were long and hard. The Victorian poet, diarist and barrister A J Munby (1828-1910)

Left: A maid ironing, 1899. **Right:** Even this 'rather modest' country house in Edenbridge, Kent, required a team of 14 servants, photographed in 1885.

held a life-long fascination for working class women, particularly those who did hard, dirty, physical labour. In 1860 he observed a scullery maid at work: 'She stood at the sink behind a wooden dresser backed with choppers and stained with blood and grease, upon which were piles of copper and saucepans that she had to scour, piles of dirty dishes that she had to wash. Her frock, her cap, her face and arms were more or less wet, soiled, perspiring and her apron was a filthy piece of sacking, wet and tied round her with a cord. The den where she wrought was low, damp, ill-smelling; windowless, lighted by a flaring gas-jet and, full in view, she had on one side a larder hung with raw meat, on the other a common urinal; besides the many ugly, dirty implements around her'.

TEN PLACES NAMED AFTER VICTORIA

Victorian architecture has become synonymous with a rich and eclectic mix of styles, which have both inspired and been reviled by critics from the start. Whatever your view, Victoria's name will forever be associated with a spectacular era of bold and often innovative buildings and structures.

351

Victoria & Albert Museum, London
This great educative museum *(right)* began life as the South Kensington Museum in 1857 housed in the 'Brompton Boilers', three industrial-looking iron sheds. Prince Albert designed the first iron 'house' himself and building work started in 1856. Reaction in the architectual press was vicious: it was described as a 'three-fold monster boiler'. The name stuck. Today's exterior building was designed by the architect of Buckingham Palace's present façade, Aston Webb. Queen Victoria laid the foundation stone in 1899 in one of her last public appearances but the museum was not opened until 1909.

352

Victoria Park in Hackney, east London. Public parks were one of the great new institutions of Victoria's age and Victoria Park, laid out by James Pennethorne in 1845 over 290 acres, was one of the earliest to benefit ordinary people in the city. It was the scene of major Chartist demonstrations in 1848.

353

Victoria Station, London, opened in 1860 as the double terminal for two of the new railway companies. Victoria was an early devotee of rail travel, one of the greatest inventions of her age.

354

Royal Victoria and Albert Docks
Two of a group of three enormous enclosed docks in east London (the third being George V Dock) built in 1855 and 1880. At the height of the British Empire these were the largest in the world and a symbol of British trade and technological superiority. They are currently subject to an ambitious regeneration scheme.

Left to right: (top left) Exterior of the Brompton Boilers by A Lanchenick, *c*1857; the Victoria & Albert museum today; The elaborate Lady Burdett-Coutts drinking fountain in Victoria Park, Hackney; Victoria, Albert and the royal family about to board an early royal train, *c*1850.

355

Victoria Tower, Palace of Westminster. This 98m (321ft) tower in Sir Charles Barry's gothic masterpiece stands to the west of the more famous clock tower (popularly known as 'Big Ben'). This was the formal entrance for the Queen to access her robing room for the State Opening of Parliament. It has become known to millions of viewers as a popular backdrop for television news reports from Parliament.

356

Royal Victoria Hospital, Netley, Hampshire. Frustrated in her inability as a woman to support her troops in battle, Victoria knitted mittens and scarves for soldiers in the Crimea. After the war she found a more direct way to look after those wounded in battle, and to train doctors and nurses for future conflict. In 1856 she laid the foundation stone for the Royal Victoria, perhaps the largest of many hospitals to bear her name during and after her lifetime. It was mostly demolished in 1966.

357

The Old Vic This venerable London theatre was originally built around 1818 and named the Royal Coburg Theatre in honour of another royal patron, Victoria's Uncle Leopold and his wife, Princess Charlotte of Wales. It was renamed the Royal Victoria Theatre in 1833 when Victoria was still a princess.

358

The former **Victoria Bridge,** London. Today called Chelsea Bridge, the original cast iron suspension bridge was founded in 1857, and later joined by its prettier neighbour, Albert Bridge. It was renamed after it was sold when its poor design threatened collapse and caused ignominy to its royal name!

359

Victoria Gaol, Hong Kong, founded in 1841, helped spread British discipline as the red ink of the British Empire spread across maps of the world. This landmark colonial building closed in recent years and is due to become the city's new arts centre.

360

'LMS 802' is the official name of Queen Victoria's last royal train – really more of a complete royal apartment on wheels with day and night saloons, kitchen and lavatory. It was built in 1869 and is now preserved in the National Railway Museum, York. Victoria took her first royal train journey as early as 1842. By the time the LMS 802 was built, Prime Minister Disraeli said that 'without the royal train there would be no great railway in Britain'. Victoria's final journey in her coffin, from Cowes, Isle of Wight to Victoria station and then from Paddington to Windsor took place – appropriately enough for the age – in a train.

TEN VICTORIAN CONVENTIONS

Several historians have argued that the popular view of stodgy Victorian morality is largely a modern fiction and that they had just as good (or bad) a time as we do today. What is certainly true is that many in Victorian society liked to see themselves as highly virtuous and above their neighbours – social distinction was everything.

361

Covering piano legs for fear of young ladies' modesty – sadly this is a wonderful (sub)-urban myth taken up by the English with glee as a joke after an Englishman reported seeing such prudery at a ladies' seminary in Niagara Falls, just at the beginning of Victoria's reign.

362

Rules Victorians loved to codify and publish rules for something that had worked perfectly well for years before and sport was a prime example. The village and town game of football (admittedly a pretty rough pastime, with no tackle too hard and no referee to protect players) became the preserve of young gentlemen in public (ie, private) schools. When they could not agree on the new rules, football evolved into two distinct games, with the formation of the Football Association (soccer) in 1863 and the Rugby Football Union in 1871.

363

A woman's place is in the home, according to this well-known proverb. It may have been the ideal family arrangement for the upper and aspiring middle classes. However, in reality two-thirds of

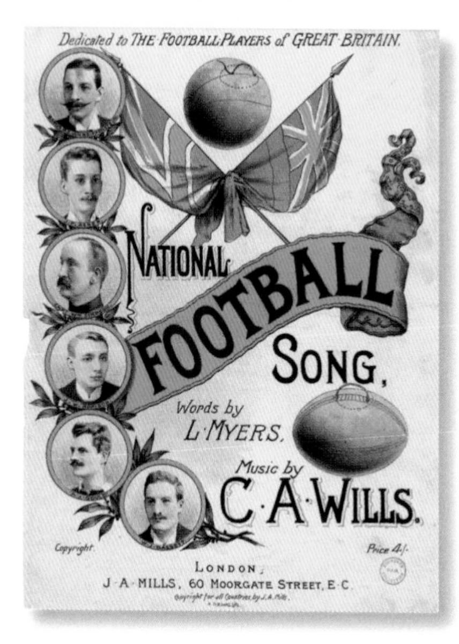

Victorian women had to go out to work, usually for long hours and as cheap labour. Queen Victoria took a dim view of female emancipation. In 1870 she wrote: 'This mad, wicked folly of "Women's Rights" with all its attendant horrors, on which her poor sex is bent, forgetting every sense of womanly feelings and propriety. Lady Amberly [a prominent feminist] ought to get a good whipping'.

364

The long arm of the law The police force, founded in 1829, came of age in Victoria's reign, policemen gaining the nickname 'Peelers' after the founder of the Metropolitan Police, Sir Robert Peel, Victoria's second Prime Minister.

365

Calling cards The seemingly absurd and elaborate ritual of sending printed cards with one's name on to the homes of neighbours of the same social scale – usually via a servant on foot – was a vital way of keeping in contact within a social circle.

366

Public lavatories Sir Samuel Peto established the first male public convenience in Fleet Street in London in 1852, not long after a new public health act. A women's lavatory was also provided, but this proved exceptional as women were not expected to stray far from home. Some even felt a women's public lavatory was improper!

Opposite page **Top:** A long line of police, *c*1829-64. **Bottom:** Sheet music cover for 'The National Football Song', *c*1880. This page **Top left:** advertisement for macassar oil, *c*1900. **Below:** The unsinkable Captain Webb, celebrated on a matchbox cover, *c*1875. **Right:** The discovery of another victim of Jack the Ripper *c*1889.

367

The antimacassar No respectable Victorian home would be without one of these lacy covers draped over the back of each armchair and sofa, to avoid men's macassar hair oil (from pressed coconut or palm) from staining the abundant upholstery of the sitting room.

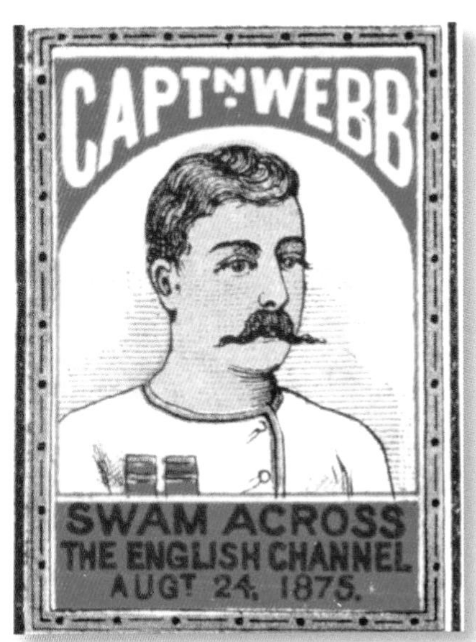

368

Swimming Previously, the ability to swim was considered coarse or at least odd; even sailors were deterred from learning. Then, with the rise of the Victorian railways and seaside resorts, swimming became a pastime and began to be taught. Most famously, the unsinkable Captain Webb was the first person to swim the English Channel in 1875 and went on to write *The Art of Swimming.*

369

Sleaze and scandal Beneath their prim and proper exterior, many Victorians relished a blood-thirsty or sleazy 'news' story as much as readers today. The now defunct *News of the World* was first published in 1843, leading with a horrifying story about a woman's murder.

370

'Lie back and think of England' This infamous quotation was supposedly said by Queen Victoria in 1858 to prepare her young daughter Princess Vicky for her wedding night. It was in fact said later, by an Edwardian lady aristocrat. Though there were many conventions about marriage and duty to guide the 'upper orders', many Victorians enjoyed sex and were successful at child rearing. In her diary, Victoria revealed that she enjoyed her physical relationship with Albert.

TEN GREAT SCIENTISTS

From developing the theory of evolution to inventing the first primitive computer, from pioneering the use of antiseptic to analysing the 'greenhouse effect', the Victorian era produced an extraordinary and eclectic mix of male and female scientists.

371

Mary Fairfax Somerville (1780-1872) Early widowhood plus a comfortable inheritance were the making of this leading scientific writer, astronomer and educator. In 1826 she presented a paper to the Royal Society, the only woman apart from the astronomer Caroline Herschel to do so. Her 1834 book, *On the Connection of the Physical Sciences* drew attention to the underlying links between disciplines, and led to the general term 'scientist' being coined.

372

Charles Babbage (1791-1871) This British mathematician was a pioneer of computing. A bright but sickly child, Babbage was educated mainly at home, developing a passion for mathematics, which he studied at Cambridge University. During the 1820s Babbage created his 'difference machine' which could perform mathematical calculations, going on to develop (although not complete) the more complex 'Analytical Engine', a revolutionary device intended to calculate and store information in a memory unit.

373

Michael Faraday (1791-1867) The annual 'Christmas Lectures' given every year to this day at the Royal Institution of Great Britain were founded in 1826 by Faraday, the British-born chemist and physicist who made a huge contribution to the study of electromagnetism and electrochemistry. In 1831 he discovered electromagnetic induction, the principle behind the electric transformer and generator. This was a crucial discovery that allowed electricity to be harnessed into a powerful new technology.

374

Mary Anning (1799-1847) Anning was born into a poverty-stricken family of fossil hunters in Lyme Regis, who sold their finds to earn a living. Yet Mary's keen eye, self-taught understanding of anatomy and business sense, meant she had become by 1838 'the greatest fossilist the world ever knew'. Her most important discovery was of the plesiosaur. However, despite the respect she earned from scientific contemporaries, many of her remarkable finds ended up unaccredited in museum and personal collections.

375

Charles Darwin (1809-82) The instigator of one of the biggest controversies to divide Victorian England and who transformed the way we think about the world today. Darwin was born into a wealthy Shropshire family (his maternal grandfather was china manufacturer Josiah Wedgwood), Darwin chose to study medicine at Edinburgh, switching to divinity at Cambridge. Following a five-year scientific trip aboard the HMS *Beagle*, he spent the next 20 years developing his theory of evolution before publishing *On The Origins of the Species by Natural Selection.*

Opposite page **Top:** Michael Faraday commemorated by John Eyre, 1886. **Bottom:** An elderly Charles Darwin. This page **Top:** A satire on London's polluted water supply, 'Death's Dispensary', 1886. **Bottom:** Elizabeth Garrett Anderson, photographed by Walery *c*1880.

376

John Snow (1813-58) In August 1854 this British physician traced the source of a cholera infection to a contaminated water pump in London's Broadwick Street, proving that the disease was transmitted by water. Snow also carried out pioneering research into controlled-dose anaesthesia and in 1853 administered chloroform to Queen Victoria during the birth of Prince Leopold, and again in 1857 at the birth of her last child Beatrice.

377

John Tyndall (1820-93) This Irish physicist, author and exceptional mountain climber became famous in the 1850s for his study of diamagnetism and later studied thermal radiation. He was the first to prove the 'Greenhouse Effect' whereby water vapour in our atmosphere absorbs infrared radiation. Tyndall wrote 17 books that brought experimental physics to a wider audience, and was Professor of Physics at the Royal Institution of Great Britain between 1853 and 1887.

378

Thomas Henry Huxley (1825-95) Pioneering biologist and educator, Thomas Huxley (who met Darwin in 1856) gained the nickname 'Darwin's Bulldog' for his efforts in getting Darwin's ideas more widely accepted through a series of widely publicised debates and lectures. Huxley published his own book on evolution in 1863 which further reinforced Darwin's theories.

379

Sir Joseph Lister Bt (1827-1912) was a British surgeon and pioneer of antiseptic surgery, who observed that doctors washing their hands between patients reduced the transference of germs. Lister also introduced carbolic acid (phenol) to sterilise surgical instruments and clean wounds, massively cutting post-operative death rates. In 1879, Listerine mouthwash was named in his honour, as is the bacterial genus Listeria.

380

Elizabeth Garrett Anderson (1836-1917) Anderson became the first Englishwoman to qualify as a doctor. She was forbidden entry to medical school, enrolling instead as a nursing student, studying discreetly with male students until she was barred. Elizabeth then took the Society of Apothecaries exam and qualified in 1865; in 1886 she was appointed as a medical assistant at St Mary's Dispensary in London. Determined to qualify as a doctor, she learnt French and finally gained a medical degree in Paris, but she was still refused entry to the medical profession. In 1872 she set up the New Hospital for Women (later the London School of Medicine for Women). Finally in 1876 an act was passed permitting women to enter the medical profession.

TEN FACTS ABOUT THE GREAT EXHIBITION

The 1851 exhibition in Hyde Park was the greatest show the world had ever seen – and it was largely the brainchild of Prince Albert. Created with his close adviser, Henry Cole, the hugely ambitious scheme was put together in only two years.

381

The Great Exhibition was a staggering success, a monument to Victorian ingenuity and entrepreneurial spirit. It attracted over 6 million visitors (as compared to the ill-fated Millennium Dome's 6.5 million from a population three times the size). On the exhibition's last day 53,000 visitors came through architect Joseph Paxton's vast glasshouse.

382

Although Albert was one of the principal drivers behind this unique enterprise he still had no official role beyond his personal interest in improving manufacturing. However, Victoria firmly attributed its success to her beloved husband. Albert hosted the initial planning meeting at Buckingham Palace and finally achieved the public role that he craved and deserved.

383

Joseph Paxton (1803-65) first drew up his futuristic design for the 'Crystal Palace' on a piece of scrap paper during a dull board meeting. All of the previous 245 plans had been rejected, but Paxton's design was revolutionary: cheap, simple, quick to erect and to remove. He set the stage for modern, prefabricated buildings for the next century and a half.

George Cruikshank
ALL THE WORLD GOING TO SEE THE GREAT EXHIBITION OF 1851.

Previous page **Left:** Queen Victoria arrives to open the Great Exhibition, by Augustus Butler, 1851. **Right:** Interior view of the Crystal Palace on opening day, after Joseph Nash, 1851, showing the great elm trees accommodated within the main hall, after local protesters had objected to them being felled.

This page **Left to right:** Satirist George Cruikshank's illustration of visitors flocking to the exhibition, 1851: This page Minton vase shown at the exhibition; Commemorative Staffordshire pot lid by T J and J Mayer; 'Bradford Court', the textiles and woollens section of the exhibition.

384

Due to the exhibition building's vast size and glazed design, ten mature elm trees on its Hyde Park site were left growing inside in response to a local outcry.

385

The Crystal Palace was approximately 563m (1,848ft) long and 124m (408ft) wide and was the largest enclosed space in the world in its time. The site filled 9.31 hectares (23 acres). It was more than three times the length of St Paul's Cathedral and had 300,000 panes of hand-blown glass.

386

Queen Victoria was fascinated by her husband's great achievement and visited the exhibition almost every other day for three months. For her, as for millions of her subjects who would never travel abroad, it was an opportunity to explore the whole world in a day.

387

Entrance tickets were cannily varied in price and ranged from a top price season ticket of 3 guineas 'for gentlemen' - equivalent to more than £2,000 today – down to a day ticket priced at one shilling. The exhibition made a large, but unintended, £186,000 profit, which was used to found the various museums of South Kensington.

388

Over 100,000 exhibits filled 1,500 pages of the official catalogue. These included: R Hall's boots of elastic enamelled cloth for tender feet…Isidore and Brandt's white wig with the arms of England formed by work in hair…an early fax machine…a stuffed Maharajah's elephant with Howdah…an 80-blade penknife…the 'Tempest Prognosticator', a barometer using leeches…a vase made of mutton fat and lard…and a bed that tipped its occupant out when it was time to get up!

389

The Queen herself exhibited the famous Koh-i-nûr diamond, whilst more prosaically, Prince Albert showed samples of wheat, oats and beans grown on the royal farm at Windsor. He also displayed real-built examples of new model social housing at the barracks opposite the exhibition – a personal passion of his.

390

When after just six months it was all over, it was *not* all over. There was much public debate about what to do with what was now a monumental white elephant (including imaginatively converting it into a 1,000-foot high glass skyscraper). Albert secretly supported plans to demolish it, but three years later it was rebuilt in the suburb of Sydenham, bigger than before, where it became a prototype 'theme park' for the masses, devoted to the arts and sciences. Sadly, it burnt down in 1936.

TEN POPULAR DISHES INSPIRED BY QUEEN VICTORIA

By the mid-19th century there had been a revolution in the domestic kitchen. Cookery authors such as Mrs Beeton brought in new recipes and ideas for home economy. The age also enjoyed new convenience items such as tinned and frozen food, the first chic, new, branded products and the arrival of fish and chips and curries.

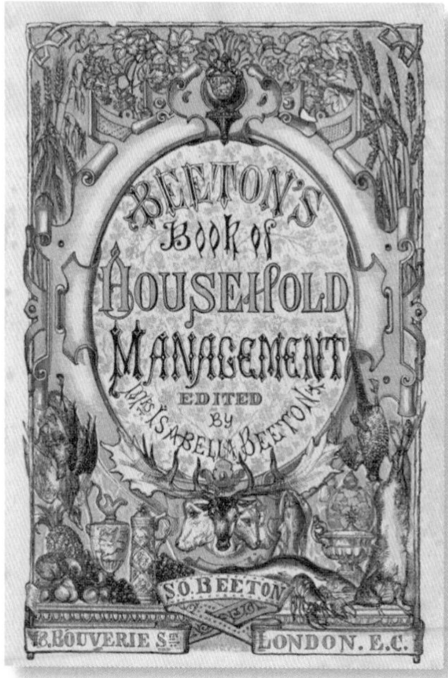

BEETON'S
Book of
HOUSEHOLD
MANAGEMENT
EDITED
BY
MRS ISABELLA BEETON
S.O. BEETON
248. BOUVERIE St.
LONDON. E.C.

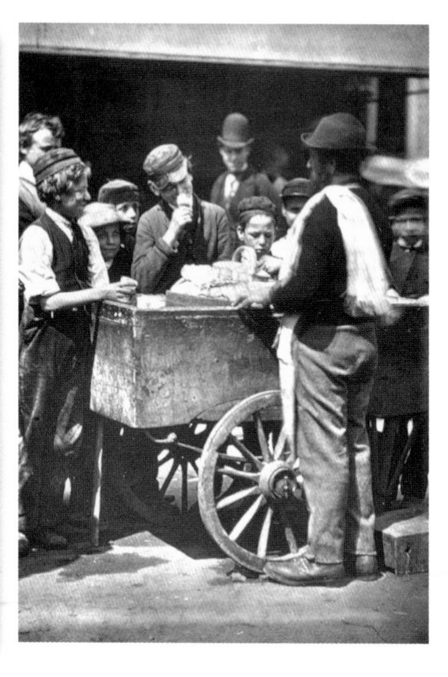

391

Royal posset, 1877 White wine and Robinson's Patent Groats (hulled cereal grains, such as oats). Good for a cold, claimed its creator Charles Francatelli, the Queen's Chef in Ordinary and Chef de Cuisine at that Victorian bastion of London society, the Reform Club.

392

Mock turtle soup No mock turtles were harmed during the making of Mrs Beeton's economical version of this very royal soup. Despite the weeping 'Mock Turtle' pictured in *Alice's Adventure's in Wonderland,* the chief ingredient of the soup is half a calf's head!

393

Macaroni à la Reine In her book *Modern Cooking for Private Families,* Eliza Acton firmly aimed at the burgeoning middle classes of Victorian England. Her recipe of 1855 is essentially good old macaroni cheese, made more 'royal' by using white Stilton for the sauce.

394

Queen cakes Far more frequently found than Victoria sponge cake in the many new Victorian cookery books, queen cakes were a staple of the Victorian high tea or taken with an evening drink. These little buns were enlivened with dried fruit soaked in brandy.

395

Partridges à la Reine The Queen's chef Francatelli recommended this suitably rich dish which no doubt groaned on the Reform Club's dining tables: boned partridges stuffed with minced game and truffles, braised and served in a dark sauce.

396

Victoria soup 'The only soup eaten by the Queen', so her chef Francatelli claimed. This beige concoction of sieved pearl barley cooked in veal stock with cream fits our pre- (and mis-) conceptions of Victorian blandness. However, the mass of Victorians also relished such

Left to right: The mournful 'Mock Turtle' in Arthur Rackham's illustration from the 1907 edition of *Alice's Adventures in Wonderland;* The original title page from Mrs Beeton's household bible, 1861; A London ice-cream vendor, photographed by John Thomson, 1877; The correct way to serve Victoria sandwiches, in neatly stacked slices shown second to top left on this page of Victorian delights.

modern fare as penny ices and spicy curries, fish and chips and tinned fruit!

397

Sandwich Victoria Tiny squares of brown bread and butter filled with slices of boiled eggs, salad and anchovy fillets. Perfect for the tea table at Osborne.

398

Marrow toast à la Victoria Francatelli advises his lady readers to have the butcher spare them the 'awkward affair' of breaking the bones for their marrow. This is lightly cooked 'with a mere suspicion of shallot' and served on squares of dry toast . It was, according to him, 'eaten every day at dinner by the Queen'.

399

Pudding Victoria Simply steam together marrow, jam, apples, cherries, peel and spices in a muslin for an hour or so and serve with a sauce. Royal chef Francatelli is uncharacteristically silent on the matter of whether his pudding amused Her Majesty.

400

Victoria sandwich (or sponge as we call it today). Mrs Beeton published this classic cake recipe in 1861, the year of Albert's death, and it was reportedly enjoyed at tea at Osborne. She recommended using jam or marmalade filling and serving it in neatly stacked slices. (See also Fact 466)

'Celebrating' the rituals of death was practically a national pastime. Even the poorest Victorians found black mourning cloth to tie around their arms, while the rich all but bankrupted themselves in funeral costs. The afterlife also held a grim fascination: attending séances or evoking gothic ghost stories were popular ways to spend an evening.

401

On the death of a loved one, everyone immediately changed into mourning clothes. The style varied according to the closeness of your relationship and then changed as time passed. Full black for immediate family gave way to mauve and lilac and grey or even black and white stripes

402

Mourning accessories were an essential requirement. There was a roaring trade in jet (black fossilised coal) for necklaces, earrings and other items. The hair of the deceased was often made into little picture keepsakes, preserved forever in the shape of feathers or drooping ferns.

403

It seems macabre to us, but grieving Victorians thought it entirely fitting to use the new fangled invention of photography to immortalise their dearly departed. Bodies were carefully dressed and propped up in a sitting position, preserved forever as if they'd just dozed off for a moment.

404

One-stop mourning warehouses, such as Jay's 'London General Mourning' provided everything needed to mourn correctly, on any budget. Shop assistants, well versed in the etiquette involved, were on hand to advise customers of the required level of mourning attire

405

Mutes were very popular at Victorian funerals. Rather like hired mourners they would add an impressive extra level of gloom standing in black-clad silence and solemn faces. In *Oliver Twist,* Oliver is hired out by Mr Sowerberry, the undertaker, to act as a mute at children's funerals, on account of the *'expression of melancholy on his face'.*

406

The stereotypical image of the drunken grave digger was a common feature of the Victorian era and no wonder. Their job was so horrible – often digging through dead bodies to make room for the new ones – that a popular way to deal with it was to be constantly inebriated.

Opposite page **Top:** An advert for Jay's 'General Mourning Warehouse', London, 1885. **Bottom:** Families enjoying a spooky evening of table moving at a spiritualist séance in 1853. **This page:** French illusionist Henri Robin and ghostly friend, in a double-exposed publicity photograph by Eugène Thiébault, 1863.

407

Cremation began to be regarded as a more acceptable – and sanitary – method of disposal, and the first crematorium opened in Woking, Surrey in 1885. However, a fear remained of being burned alive, so in some places cremation was delayed to reassure relatives.

408

As the population increased, large cemeteries were built on the outskirts of London to keep pace. There was even a platform at Waterloo station known as 'Necropolis station' where a train took coffins directly to the suburban cemetery at Brookwood in Surrey. The train was divided according to faith and class so even in death one was with the 'right' people.

409

Attending a séance was a popular way to spend an evening and various famous 'seers' made the fashionable circuit, appearing to communicate with the dead. Despite many mediums being exposed as fraudsters, the belief in communicating with the afterlife remained.

410

We have the Victorians to blame (or thank!) for many of the ghost stories we tell today. The era saw a burgeoning of terrible tales as part of the Victorian love affair with the macabre, with faked up, double-exposed photographs offered as spine tingling 'proof'.

'Off with their heads!' Victoria must have been extremely unamused by this wicked caricature that appeared on the cover of the French satirical magazine *Le Rire* (The Laugh) of 1897, in 'honour' of her Diamond Jubilee.

VICTORIA'S IMAGE

Her secluded childhood at Kensington Palace had kept Victoria shielded from public view; her accession to the throne sparked a proliferation of imagery of the young Queen which, due to technological advances, could be distributed more widely than ever before. Franz Xaver Winterhalter painted numerous portraits of Queen Victoria, Prince Albert and their children. His paintings, alongside portraits by Sir George Hayter, John Partridge, Sir Edwin Landseer and later Heinrich von Angeli, and numerous photographers and sculptors helped to shape Victoria's public persona.

Family formed an integral part of Queen Victoria's public image. Popular prints of the Queen and Prince Albert were circulated widely around the time of their marriage in 1840; as the children grew, these images depicted a happy family playing games and having fun together. However, as Victoria aged – and particularly following her prolonged withdrawal from public life after Prince Albert's death – some sections of the British press grew less sycophantic. Various satirical and political cartoonists took swipes at the ageing monarch, with the French press being especially venomous!

TEN ADULT PORTRAITS

Queen Victoria's likeness was recorded by scores of artists and photographers. Some of these images were more intimate portraits intended for friends and family, but the Queen also placed great emphasis on disseminating a carefully constructed image of herself to her subjects.

411

Queen Victoria by Franz Xaver Winterhalter, 1843 *(above)* This alluring portrait was painted for Victoria as a present to Prince Albert on his 24th birthday. She called it her 'secret picture'; with her hair hanging loose across her naked shoulder, it was a portrait meant for his eyes only. Victoria later described it as 'my darling Albert's favourite picture'.

412

Self-portrait, 1845 *(below)* Victoria drew a number of self-portraits as a child (see pages 12-15) but few as an adult. This pencil study of her face was made shortly before her 26th birthday. She had been on the throne for eight years, and the face in the mirror already shows the determination, perhaps stubbornness, of a young woman feeling the strain of the speed of change and the weight of responsibility in her life. It is inscribed in her hand, 'Ball dress May 19 – [18]45'.

413

Queen Victoria by Franz Xaver Winterhalter, 1847 *(shown on page 23)* The Queen is depicted wearing her wedding veil and wreath of orange blossom and the diamond and sapphire brooch given to her by Prince Albert on the eve of their wedding. The portrait was commissioned by the Queen and presented to the Prince on their seventh wedding anniversary.

414

Queen Victoria by Brian Edward Duppa, 5 July 1854 *(far left)* Victoria and Albert were important patrons and collectors of the new art of photography, and commissioned hundreds of images of family and friends. Victoria commissioned this portrait as a surprise for her husband. It shows her holding a framed photograph of Albert taken by the same photographer a few months earlier.

415

Queen Victoria by Charles-Lucien-Louis Muller, 1856 *(below)* This study was made for the large picture painted by Muller for Napoleon III to record the Queen's arrival at St Cloud – his chateau in France – in 1855. Victoria described the visit: 'In a blaze of light…we reached the Palace. The dear Empress, Princess Mathilde, & the Ladies received us at the door & took us up a beautiful staircase lined with the splendid Cent Gardes.'

416

Queen Victoria by John Jabez Edwin Mayall, 15 May 1860 *(over page)* This photographic session, commissioned by the Queen, was the

first occasion that photographs of Victoria had ever been published. The public had never been able to buy a photograph of their sovereign before and the images were extremely popular.

417

Queen Victoria by Heinrich von Angeli, 1875 *(right)* In April 1875, the Queen wrote to her daughter Victoria recording the progress of this portrait: 'a marvellous likeness – as if I looked at myself in the glass'. The finished work was sent over to Berlin so that her daughter could see it. She wrote: 'Your beautiful picture has arrived and is safe in my room! How very like it is. If I had any thing to object in so fine a portrait, I would say…that it looks a trifle stern and set'. 'I think', wrote the Queen in response, 'that for a picture to represent the Queen it was necessary to have it serious – and I constantly begged him to make it so'.

418

Queen Victoria by Charles Knight, 1887 *(shown on page 24)* A rare portrait of the Queen smiling, taken in her Golden Jubilee year. Photographs and paintings of the Queen in later life invariably show her looking solemn or melancholic, so this is a very surprising and unusual image. Victoria's Golden Jubilee was a grand, national celebration, and after many years of mourning the Queen resumed some public duties.

419

Queen Victoria Diamond Jubilee portrait by William and Daniel Downey, 1893 *(right)* This photograph, commissioned by the Queen, was used as an official portrait for her Diamond Jubilee in 1897 but was actually taken in July 1893 on the occasion of the wedding of her grandson, Prince George (later King George V) and Princess Victoria Mary of Teck.

420

Queen Victoria in spectacles, by an unknown photographer, late 1890s *(below)* An informal portrait of Victoria as an elderly lady. The Queen once exclaimed: 'God knows there is nothing to admire in my ugly old person'.

WE ARE NOT AMUSED!

Victoria got off quite lightly as a subject for British satirical artists, although there was some sniping, particularly at her long withdrawal from public life after Albert's death. French cartoonists, however, were not so kind!

421
A ghostly Queen Elizabeth I appears to Victoria. 'Why do you frown, what have I done?' asks Victoria. 'Let grief prevail o'er duty', the disapproving spectre replies, in this 1869 comment on Victoria's extended mourning.

422
The aptly named *Hornet* cartoons usually had a sting in their tail. The sentiment in this one seems to be mainly benign. Captioned 'A late valentine - better late than never', the cartoon is dated 27 February 1872. On this day, Victoria and the Prince of Wales were warmly received when they attended a public parade through London and a grand service of thanksgiving in St Paul's cathedral following Edward's recovery from illness.

423
'Her Resolute Opposition - a poor old broom against the New Flood' depicts Victoria helpless trying to stem the tide of Irish Home Rule in 1878. The faces of Prime Minister Gladstone and Irish reformer and nationalist politician Charles Stewart Parnell can be seen bubbling up in the crashing waves.

424
By 1896 Victoria had become England's longest reigning monarch (far *too* long, in French opinon!). She is spied on by her Colonial Secretary, Joseph Chamberlain,

THE RAZOR; OR, LONDON HUMORIST AND SATIRIST. [JULY 11, 1868.

A VISION.

V——"WHY DO YOU FROWN—WHAT HAVE I DONE?" E——"LET GRIEF PREVAIL O'ER DUTY!"

THE HORNET.

FEBRUARY 27TH, 1872.

A LATE VALENTINE—AND BETTER LATE THAN NEVER.

"HER RESOLUTE OPPOSITION."
A Poor Old Broom Against the New Flood.

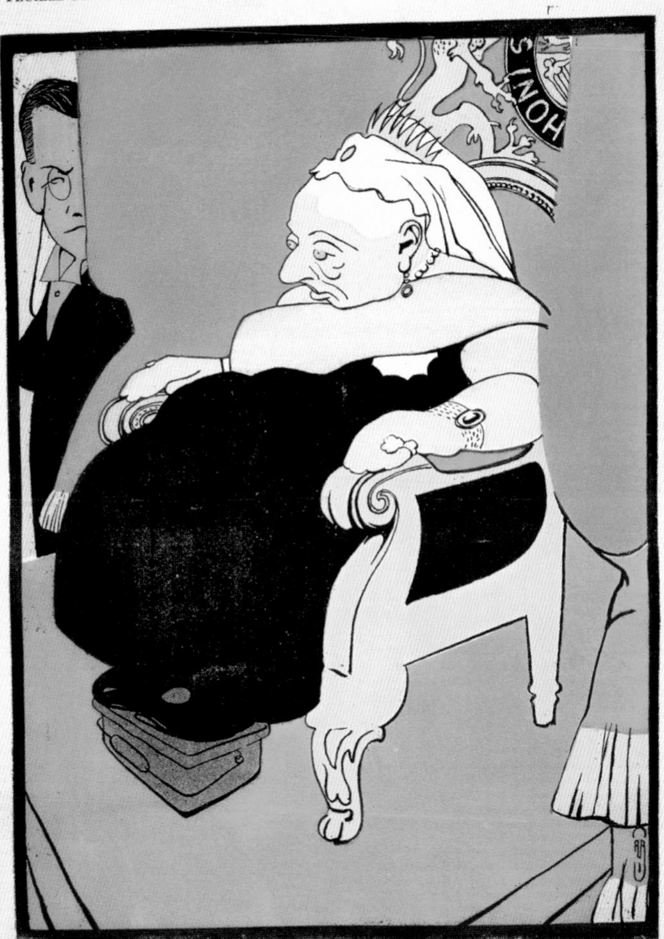

from behind the throne curtain. This is one of a set of 13 lithographic satirical posters, called *Le Musée de Sires, Feuilles de Caricatures Politiques* (Museum of Lords or Rulers, sheets of political caricatures) by the engraver and painter Auguste Roubille, published in 1900.

425

At first glance this 1878 illustration from French arts magazine *Cocorico*, of a poorly Victoria being offered comfort

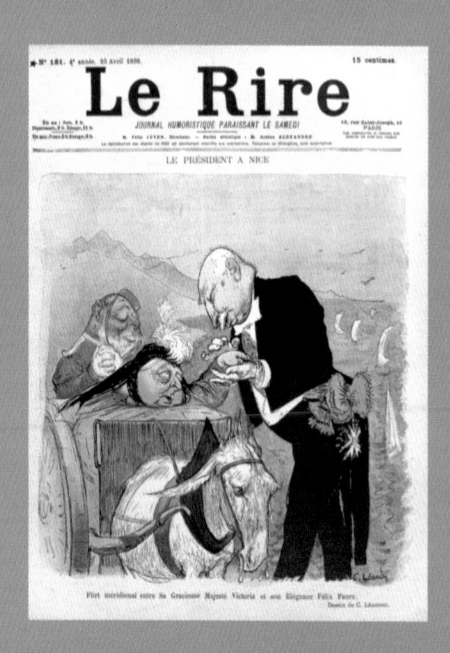
★ N° 181. 4ᵉ année. 23 Avril 1898. 15 centimes.

Le Rire

JOURNAL HUMORISTIQUE PARAISSANT LE SAMEDI

PARIS

LE PRÉSIDENT A NICE

Flirt méridional entre Sa Gracieuse Majesté Victoria et son Élégance Félix Faure.

Dessin de C. Léandre.

seems fairly innocent, but it has a sinister message. The 'kindly gent' with the rifle is Paul Kruger, President of the Transvaal Republic, South Africa, and he is offering the Queen the 'dum dum' bullets, rather than cough sweets. These expanding bullets caused catastrophic injury and were used by British troops early in the Boer War, despite strong European disapproval. Their use was banned in international warfare by the Hague Convention in 1899.

426

(Shown on page 124). A less-than-flattering commemorative issue of the French humorous magazine *Le Rire* ('The Laugh') for the Queen's Diamond Jubilee in 1897, shows her with a shining crown atop a sad old face.

427

Queen Victoria appears in a bathing machine on holiday in Nice. The Prince of Wales is shown following behind in a porter's uniform while his elderly mother flirts with the French President Félix Faure. This cover of April 1898 comments on the start of *L'Entente Cordiale* (usually translated as 'friendly understanding') between Britain and France.

428

John Brown, manservant and close friend to the Queen in her later years (some claimed he was more than that!) hovers in the background holding a towel, as Victoria reads The Bible in the bath, looking rather perplexed. She has made paper boats from other publications, including the *Daily Chronicle*. The image, drawn by Tiret-Bognet, comes from *Le Rire*, dated 1899.

429

'Please help a poor widow with a large family', reads the sign held by the elderly Queen, sitting on the steps of Buckingham Palace with the Prince of Wales and the rest of her royal brood maintained on the Civil List. They hold their upturned coronets out to 'John Bull' (representing the British Government). This cartoon by Frederick Opper appeared in an issue of the US humorous magazine *Puck* published from 1871 to 1916. A London edition appeared briefly between 1889 and 1890.

430

Finally, we couldn't resist this cheeky 1970s advertisement. The rotund Queen, still going strong, enjoys a box of after-dinner mints!

Right: Princess Louise's statue of her mother in coronation robes. Opposite page **Top:** The 'Victoria' hoodoo in Bryce Canyon National Park US. **Centre:** Dublin's 'auld bitch', now in Sydney, Australia. **Bottom:** Formerly in a grand Hong Kong square, this statue of Victoria awaits repair in a Japanese scrap yard in 1947.

431

Kensington Palace, London
In 1893, the Queen returned to the place of her birth and unveiled a white marble statue, carved from a model created by her daughter Princess Louise. Passing through the cheering crowds, her grand-daughter remarked that she must feel very proud. 'No', replied the queen, 'very humble'.

432

Leinster House, Dublin James Joyce called the statue of Queen Victoria outside Leinster House 'the auld bitch' but it survived when most other signs of royalty were removed in the 1920s. In July 1948, as Ireland moved towards its final break with the Crown, the statue was unceremoniously winched off its perch and carted away to obscurity and abandonment. It was rediscovered after a long search in the 1980s, covered with moss. Like many things Irish, this Victoria eventually emigrated to Australia, and now enjoys a new and better appreciated life in Sydney.

433

Aden, Yemen The statue of Queen Victoria in Aden was winched by crane over the wall of the British Embassy in 1967 lest a revolutionary mob tear it to pieces as Britain beat a hasty retreat. Recently she was reinstated to preside once again over a dusty park in this remote former outpost of empire.

TEN STATUES OF VICTORIA WORLDWIDE

Almost every large town in Britain has a statue of Queen Victoria, raised when her personality became firmly embedded in the national consciousness. Those spread over her far-flung empire have fared less well. But long after most statues of British kings and administrators have been toppled or removed, Queen Victoria often survives.

434

Winchester Hall, UK Winchester's statue, far too important to be kept outside is perhaps the most evocative, grandiose and monumental sculpture, portraying Queen Victoria as elderly and sunken under the weight of her own destiny.

435

Cape Town, South Africa Touches of this city's Victorian elegance remain everywhere, including the neo-classical Parliament House, with the statue of the Queen untouched through generations of political change.

436

Quebec City, Canada Separatists blew up the statue of Queen Victoria in Quebec City in 1963. Her head was separated from her body; both now sit in display cases in the Musée de la Civilisation. Plans are afoot to restore her.

437

Hong Kong In 1896 a magnificent stone dome surmounted a statue of the Queen erected in a grand square in Hong Kong. During the Japanese occupation in World War II, she disappeared, and at the end of the war was discovered in a scrap yard in Japan, awaiting the smelter. She was returned to Hong Kong and repaired. However, like her empire, the monumental dome protecting her has gone and the royal head is now exposed to the eroding power of the elements.

438

Bryce Canyon, US Hardly a statue, but a natural phenomenon known as a hoodoo. Two hundred million years of erosion have sculpted many figures in the limestone of the area, this one with an uncanny resemblance to the Queen. Its discoverer, Ebenezer Bryce, described the intricate, beautiful canyon as 'a hell of a place to lose a cow'.

439

Victoria Memorial, London
The approach to Buckingham Palace is graced by a huge monument to the Queen by Thomas Brock, unveiled by her grandson the German Kaiser in 1911. It is nearly 23m (75ft) high and used 2,300 tons of white marble. Victoria sits at the centre, surmounted by a gilded figure of Victory, and is flanked by her carved handmaidens Courage and Constancy. Sir Osbert Sitwell was less impressed, describing it as 'tons of allegorical females in white wedding cake marble, with whole litters of their cretinous children'.

440

Victoria Memorial, Kolkata, India
The grandiose Victoria Memorial in the city once known as Calcutta is not just a statue, but a huge monumental building that is a veritable shrine to Queen Victoria. It remains carefully maintained as a major landmark while elsewhere in the former Indian empire, her statues now lie defaced in yards, or sit as curiosities in museums.

VICTORIA ON SCREEN

Young, old, sentimental, sensational… Queen Victoria has often been portrayed in film and television, from leading roles to cartoon voiceovers. Here are ten actresses who brought Victoria to life in different ways.

441

Anna Neagle in *Victoria the Great* (1937), director Herbert Wilcox. This wildly successful production launched Neagle's career in the States. It follows Victoria's courtship and marriage, a highlight being the thrilling assassination attempt in which her life is saved by Prince Albert. The sequel, *Sixty Glorious Years* followed hot on the heels of this blockbuster.

442

Beryl Mercer (a cameo role) in *The Little Princess* (1939), director Walter Lang. There's not a dry eye left in the house as the kindly Queen Victoria saves the day as Sara Crewe (Shirley Temple) searches desperately for her father.

443

Irene Dunn in *The Mudlark* (1950), director Jean Negulesco. Also starring Alec Guinness as a wonderful Disraeli, this fictionalised account of how the Queen emerged from her secluded mourning in 1875 thanks to a starving urchin was a big hit in Britain.

444

Patricia Routledge in 'Victoria Regina' (1964), director Stuart Latham. Based on Laurence Housman's play, the splendid Routledge played Victoria ageing from 19 to 80 over four episodes of this BBC mini series.

445

The voice of **Eve Brenner** as the Mouse Queen in *The Great Mouse Detective* (1986, animation), director Ron Clements. The heroes are the mice of Victorian London, where the Mouse Queen is celebrating her Diamond Jubilee alongside (or really, underfoot) the 'real' Queen Victoria.

446

Miriam Margolyes as Victoria in 'Blackadder's Christmas Carol' (1988), director Richard Boden. In this Christmas episode Victoria and Albert (Jim Broadbent) do a hilarious double-act as a couple of rather frisky, middle-aged royals. Bizarrely, Victoria wears a widow's cap, although Albert is alive and well!

Left to right: Anna Neagle in 1937; Beryl Mercer (seated) in 1939; Billy Connolly and Judi Dench in 1997; Poster featuring Emily Blunt in 2009.

450

Emily Blunt in *Young Victoria* (2009), director Jean-Marc Vallée. Sumptuous costumes, mouthwatering locations and an impressive cast including Rupert Friend as Albert, Paul Bettany as Lord Melbourne and Miranda Richardson as the Duchess of Kent. While the majority of films portray the Queen as a widow, this is a highly romanticised yet very enjoyable love story of the young royal couple. Blunt is a tender, beautiful Victoria with a bit of a temper, shown meeting and falling in love with Prince Albert, who provides a rock to her during her early years on the throne. The after-show party of the film's London première was held at the real Victoria's childhood home Kensington Palace.

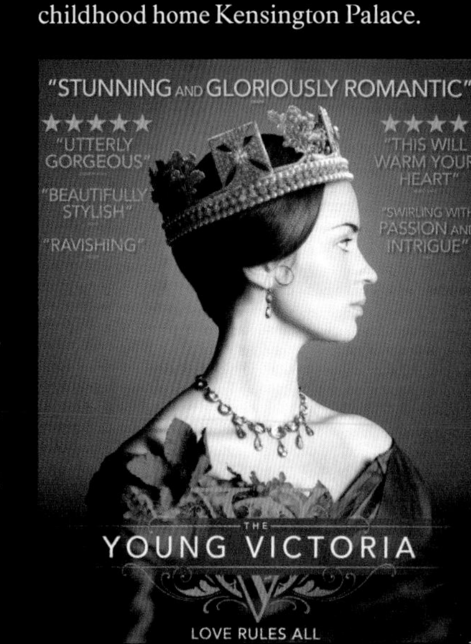

447

Judi Dench in *Mrs Brown* (1997), director John Madden. Dench's moving performance of the grieving Queen finding happiness with her late husband's ghillie (played by Billy Connolly) won her a BAFTA (British Academy for Film and Television Arts Award), and the film was nominated for an Oscar.

448

Victoria Hamilton in 'Victoria and Albert' (2001), director John Erman. This BBC mini series also starred Jonathan Firth as a rather stuffy, reluctant Albert, warmed up by Hamilton's girlish exuberance as the couple develop a loving marriage. A great cast of schemers and supporters included David Suchet, Diana Rigg and Peter Ustinov as an elderly and blustering William IV.

449

Pauline Collins as the Queen in the Dr Who episode 'Tooth and Claw' (2006). In this episode the Doctor (David Tennant) and Rose (Billie Piper) arrive in Victorian Scotland and meet a feisty old Queen Victoria in a manor house. Victoria is game for anything; unfazed by Rose's mini-skirt and the Doctor's dire warnings. Soon werewolves appear and the intepid threesome use the Koh-i-nûr to defeat them. As you would.

VICTORIA'S LEGACY

The fact that Queen Victoria's name is still so closely associated with the 19th century is testament to her continued presence in the public psyche. She committed herself to upholding the morals and values that she and Prince Albert had deemed essential qualities of a strong monarchy. The sheer length of her reign provided a stabilising influence during a period of unprecedented social change and upheaval. Her unwavering belief in the mystique of monarchy and the importance of its relationship with the public reinforced her status as one to be revered. Victoria's relationship with the media is perhaps her most enduring legacy. While she did not actively seek to control the media, the swift changes in the production and distribution of news and imagery during her 63 years on the throne establish her as a truly modern figure. The images of her that survive around the world in art galleries, historic buildings, public sculpture and popular culture in general, guarantee she will retain this status for future generations.

Previous page: Detail from The Victoria Memorial opposite Buckingham Palace. The memorial is a landmark for many of London's visitors today. The huge white marble monument was sculpted by Thomas Brock and unveiled by Victoria's grandson the Kaiser in 1911.

This page **Left:** Prisoners on a treadwheel in Pentonville Prison, 1895. **Right:** Poster advertising Blackpool, 1890 Opposite page **Top:** Advertising card for Singer cabinet table sewing machine, 1904. **Bottom:** *The Night School*, 1892 by Edgar Bundy, depicting people studying for self improvement at the end of a long working day.

451

The prison system Social problems in prisons in the early part of the century such as gambling and prostitution gave rise in the 1840s to a desire to reform the service to focus on moral regeneration of inmates. However, while hard labour and solitude in single cells would keep prisoners out of trouble, the notion of rehabilitation remained a long way off.

452

Cremation 'No scents or balsams are needed, as on Greek or Roman piles, to overcome the noxious effluvia of a corpse burned in the open air.' Sir Henry Thompson, writing in *The Contemporary Review* in January 1834, was one of the first people to advocate cremation as an alternative to burial, as urban cemeteries became increasingly overcrowded. It was legalised in 1884. (See Fact 407)

453

Mass communication London's Great Western Railway began using the

TEN WAYS VICTORIANS CHANGED THE WAY WE LIVE TODAY

Many Victorian innovations were precursors to the modern amenities we know today. Industrialisation and rapid expansion of cities required creative solutions to problems arising from dramatic social and economic change.

first commercial electrical telegraph in 1839. Advances in technology by 1897 enabled Queen Victoria to send her Diamond Jubilee message to the entire British Empire. The internet was on its way. (See also Fact 179)

454

Holidays Squalid living conditions in cities and a growing middle class with more disposable income helped to shape the concept 'getting away from it all'. The 1871 Bank Holidays Act designated four days off for workers in England, Wales and Northern Ireland, five for those in Scotland. Holidaymakers flocked to fashionable seaside resorts on rapidly expanding railways. (See also pages 92-3)

455

Celebrities Improvements in printing techniques, the creation of the daguerrotype by Louis Daguerre in 1837 and subsequent advances in photography enabled a mass production of popular imagery. Publications such as the *Illustrated London News* printed pictures of Florence Nightingale and other celebrities, and photographs of Queen Victoria and Prince Albert were widely circulated.

456

Social mobility The enormous boom in industry during the Victorian period helped some upper-middle class businessmen generate incomes that rivalled those of the aristocracy. For example, when his company was at its peak, Manchester cotton tycoon John Rylands employed 15,000 people in 17 mills and factories.

457

Inner cities The rapid growth of urban populations began in the 18th century but it was not until 1851 that, for the first time, half of the British population lived in towns. Industrial centres such as Liverpool and Manchester attracted thousands of people.

458

'Fast' fashion During the 19th century, fashionable clothing became more accessible than ever before with the mechanisation of spinning, weaving and printing of cotton, which was less expensive than silk. These developments, alongside the mid-century introduction of the sewing machine, enabled women with less money to dress fashionably and to adopt fashion trends quickly.

459

A modern sewer system Immediately following the 'Great Stink' of 1858, when the smell of untreated human excrement overwhelmed London, Parliament resolved to modernise the city's sewer system with five gigantic sewers built by a team of engineers led by Joseph Bazelgette. The result was a new underground system which directed waste out of London to the Thames Estuary. (See also Fact 216)

460

Victorian values The Victorian middle classes lived by a set of values and social ideals such as individual hard work, competition, enterprise, productivity and achievement, which they believed led to progress and set them apart from the aristocracy. A common factor of these ideals was the notion of self-help.

TEN WAYS VICTORIA'S NAME LIVES ON

An enduring favourite choice for baby girls since her reign, 'Victoria' lives on in a variety of different ways the world over, with cakes, flowers, buildings, giant water lilies and natural wonders all named in her honour.

461

Victoria plum *(above)* The most versatile of the English plums, the Victoria plum was first cultivated in Sussex in 1840. It is often known as the Queen of Plums.

462

Victoria, Australia Many hundreds of towns and whole tracts of land were named after the Queen. As British settlement in Australia increased, a new colony was separated from New South Wales in 1851 and proclaimed as the Colony – now State – of Victoria. Over 75 per cent of 'Victorians' now live in Melbourne, the state capital.

463

Victoria & Albert Museum
The greatest decorative arts museum in the world was founded in 1852, with profits from the Great Exhibition the previous year. It aimed to make works of art accessible to all, and was initially known as the Museum of Manufacture. The museum moved to its present location on the Cromwell Road, London in 1857, and in 1899 Victoria laid the foundation stone in what was to become a grand new entrance, while in a further tribute, the building was renamed the Victoria & Albert Museum in memory of Prince Albert's enthusiastic early support for the project. (See also Fact 351)

464

Victoria waterlily It was natural that when the botanist John Lindley came across an immense waterlily in South America in 1839, he should name it after the Queen. *Victoria amazonica* can grow leaves up to 3m (over 9ft) in diameter.

465

MS Queen Victoria In 1839, Samuel Cunard was awarded the contract for carrying mail across the North Atlantic. Cunard developed a prosperous passenger and cargo service and made ocean liners a success, beating many rivals. Queen Victoria created him a baronet in 1859. His company lives on, and the MS *Queen Victoria,* one of Cunard's most modern, luxurious liners perpetuates her name.

Opposite page **Left:** Victoria plums. **Top right:** The giant waterlily, *Victoria amazonica* painted in 1851. **Bottom right:** Cunard's MS *Queen Victoria.* This page **Left:** *Herd of buffalo, opposite Garden Island, Victoria Falls,* 1852 by Thomas Baines. **Inset:** Scottish explorer David Livingstone in 1864.

466

Victoria sponge Mrs Beeton's 1861 recipe for Victoria sponge includes 4 eggs, their weight in pounded sugar, a spoonful of salt, and any kind of jam or marmalade. Today's cooks would probably do better to follow the classic 110g (4oz) each of butter, caster sugar and self-raising flour, with 2 large eggs.

467

Victoria University, Wellington An act of the New Zealand parliament established this university in 1897, named in honour of Victoria's Diamond Jubilee. Motto 'Wisdom is to be more desired than gold', it specialises in law degrees.

468

The Victoria Falls Mosi-oa-Tunya or 'the smoke that thunders' in southern Africa was re-named, after explorer David Livingstone became the first European to set eyes on this natural wonder on 16 November 1855.

469

Victoria Cross Noted for its simplicity, this plain, bronze medal is the nation's highest award for bravery. It was first given in 1856 to Charles Davis Lucas, who had hurled a live shell over the side of the ship HMS *Hecla*. Since then it has been awarded 1,356 times. (See also Fact 196)

470

Avenue Victoria, Paris Victoria is immortalised in hundreds of street names in Britain and around the world, and even in Paris, a city that she visited several times. In August 1855 the Emperor Napoleon III honoured her, as she gleefully recorded in a letter to her uncle King Leopold: 'they have asked to call a new street, which we opened, after me!'

Victorian drinkers, photographed by John Thomson for *Victorian London Street Life*, 1876-7; Opposite page **Left:** *Punch* cartoon from 1876, showing Prime Minister Disraeli adding a second, grander Victoria to 'The Queen's Head' pub sign. Disraeli had been instrumental in Victoria gaining the title 'Empress of India', although not everyone approved. 'Mr Bull' comments: 'No, no, Benjamin, it will never do! You can't improve on the old "Queen's Head".' **Right:** A Victorian water tap on the bar of a London pub.

471

The Victoria, Lincoln This is an old-fashioned local near to the castle, full of pictures of the Queen, but the offer of eight constantly changing real ales, foreign draught beers and local farm cider – plus regular beer festivals – must be the main attractions.

472

The Victoria, Holkham, Norfolk An 'upmarket but informal' small hotel, owned by the Holkham Estate. The Victoria was built auspiciously in the coronation year of 1838 by Lord Leicester, in the estate village next to Holkham Hall, and looking out over beautiful north Norfolk coast and Holkham beach.

473

The Victoria, Durham An 'unchanging' family-run late 19th century local, with the full Victorian décor: loads of mahogany, etched and cut glass and mirrors, William Morris wallpaper, handsome fireplaces and many prints and engravings of Queen Victoria, together with Staffordshire figurines of the Queen and Prince Albert.

474

The Albert, Victoria St, London A magnificent gin palace that has its own 'division bell' to call Members of Parliament back to the House of Commons nearby in time to vote. Built in 1864 it is full of classic Victorian features, including

RAISE A GLASS TO VICTORIA!

Britain has hundreds of pubs named in honour of the Queen, many dating from the late 19th century and still fitted out with etched glass, mahogany bars and brass fittings. Here's a selection of old and new, most recommended as 'worth a visit' in The Good Pub Guide.

"THE QUEEN WITH TWO HEADS."

MR. BULL. "NO, NO, BENJAMIN, IT WILL NEVER DO! YOU CAN'T IMPROVE ON THE OLD '*QUEEN'S HEAD!*'"

a heavy polished dark wood bar and etched glass window.

475

The Victoria, Earl Soham, Suffolk. This remote village pub is fairly basic with well-worn kitchen tables and pews, plus several pictures of Queen Victoria and aspects of her reign. The Earl Soham micro-brewery, which is conveniently situated opposite, supplies a range of its own beers, including 'Albert Ale' and 'Victoria Bitter'.

476

The Victoria Inn, Perranuthnoe, Cornwall A busy and popular village pub with a friendly atmosphere and stunning views, according to reviewers, and just a few minutes stroll from the beaches of Mount Bay. The Victoria is reputed to be one of the oldest inns in Cornwall. Worth trying the local beers for the names alone, which include 'Doom Bar' and 'Betty Stogs'.

477

The Princess Victoria, Uxbridge Road, London Another grand gin palace. This one has been carefully restored, with a 'handsome' marble-tipped bar horseshoe bar, oil paintings, stuffed animal heads and parquet flooring.

478

The Victoria and Albert, Netherhampton, Wiltshire. A 'cosy', black-beamed bar in a simple thatched cottage, with large open fires, ancient tiled floors, genuine horse brasses, and lovely views over farmland. Handy for exploring Wilton House, home of the Pembrokes, and for walking in the Nadder Valley.

479

The Victoria, Bayswater, London. An impressive mahogany horseshoe bar with original fittings, including this water tap *(right)* originally to provide the mixer for absinthe, a favourite Victorian tipple. The place is adorned with Victorian pictures and prints, 19th-century memorabilia, cast-iron fireplaces, gilded mirrors and brass mock gas-lamps.

And finally, possibly the most famous fictional pub named after Victoria is...

480

'The Vic', in BBC1's 'EastEnders' Not the place to go for a quiet drink! The 'Queen Victoria public house' has been the scene of at least three murders, one in which a bust of the Queen herself was used as a murder weapon. Shocking! There have been countless rows, fights, seductions and abductions, and a Christmas day divorce. This iconic pub (actually a set in the BBC Elstree Centre at Borehamwood, Hertfordshire) has featured in nearly every episode since 'EastEnders' was first broadcast on 19 February 1985.

TEN VICTORIAN PRODUCTS STILL USED TODAY

Many household items were established in the 19th century, though most original names have disappeared. Nobody now remembers Eiffel Tower lemonade, Batty's Nabob Pickle or Ogden's Saratoga Whiffs (a cigarette), but a few are still with us, a testament to longevity, good marketing and their place in British hearts.

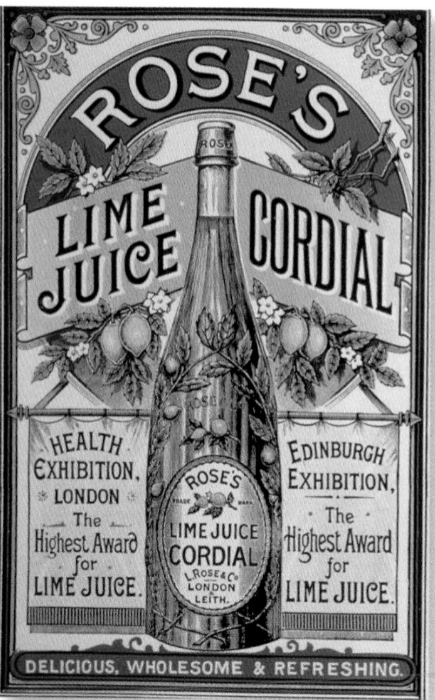

481

Bovril Bovril is older than its rival Marmite by several decades, beginning life as Johnston's Fluid Beef before being renamed in 1886. The 'beef tea' was, according to an early advertising campaign, 'a factor in our empire's strength'.

482

Rose's Lime Juice Cordial Of a plethora of tonics, cordials and drinks that jostled for public attention in the 1870s and 80s, only Rose's lime cordial is still with us, marked now as then by its pretty embossed bottles. The eye-watering lime concentrate, founded by L Rose at Leith in 1865, is still popular.

483

Bird's Custard Bird's custard was one of the first products created in the Victorian age, when Alfred Bird formulated eggless custard in 1837, because his wife was allergic to eggs. Its blue and yellow packaging is now one of the most recognisable British brands.

484

Cadbury's Cocoa Cadbury's empire (now owned by US giant Kraft) began in 1824 when a Birmingham Quaker grocer named John Cadbury began experimenting with crushed cocoa beans and hot milk. By 1842 he was selling 11 sorts of cocoa and 16 sorts of drinking chocolate. However, the business really took off in 1862 when he imported a Dutch cocoa press. This removed the cocoa butter from the beans, so the resulting powder was far more tasty.

485

Eno's Fruit Salts In 1850, Crossley Eno first sold his fruit salt, essentially bicarbonate of soda. Its enduring charm remains the miraculous, instantaneous fizz, followed by a large, satisfying burp.

486

Lyle's Golden Syrup In 1881 Abram Lyle and his five sons set up a sugar refinery in London. Not content to discard the

treacly by-product of sugar refining, the Lyles processed this sticky goo further to produce a light coloured liquid. Two years later their distinctive Golden Syrup appeared. The gold and green label and paint-tin lid have perhaps changed least of all Victorian brands.

487

Oxo Liebig's Extract of Meat might not have made it into the 20th century as a brand name, but in the 1890s, as the competition sharpened its teeth, the company shortened its name to something catchier – 'Lemco'. In 1900 they shortened it further, perfectly capturing the essence of their product – and Oxo was born.

488

Garibaldi biscuits The thin wafer-like biscuit, excellent for dunking in tea but reminiscent of squashed flies to generations of children, was named in honour of the Italian patriot Giuseppe Garibaldi, who toured England in 1854 and was received with great enthusiasm.

489

Sunlight Soap Sunlight was a pioneering product – marketed and packaged from 1884 as single bars by the Lever Brothers in an era when soap was cut like cheese to the requisite length in shops. After a long, slow decline in popularity, production ceased in Britain in 2009 but the brand lives on in a number of countries around the world.

490

Camp Coffee Love it or loathe it, Camp Coffee has clung tenaciously to the supermarket shelves, surviving the rise of modern granulated instant brands and the snobbishness of 'real' coffee. Robert Campbell Paterson founded a company making pickles and chutney in 1849, but later created the liquid coffee. It was popular with the Gordon Highlanders in India, who appeared on the distinctive label, though the Indian manservant has been promoted gradually and the men now sit together to drink their coffee.

TEN WAYS TO LIVE (AND DIE!) LIKE A VICTORIAN TODAY

While many of the Victorians' favourite pastimes and leisure pursuits remain prevalent today, there are many hidden gems to discover.

491

Post a letter in a Victorian Penfold letter box. John Wornham Penfold's 1866 pillar box was a simple hexagonal shape decorated with acanthus leaves and scrolled 'VR' letters for Victoria Regina. The design of its distinctive six-sided cap was based on the ancient Tower of the Winds in Athens. From 1874, the 'Penfold' was manufactured in the new standard colour, (pillar box) red.

492

Strike a pose for a Victorian-style portrait. The Olde Victorian Picture House on Llandudno pier provides Victorian-style costumes but uses modern technology to produce black and white photographs so you don't have to stand still for ages like the Victorians did. With extraordinarily long exposure times, it's not suprising that people didn't often smile in their formal portraits. You try saying cheese for over a minute!

493

Visit a bath house From 1897, the Royal Baths in Harrogate impressed Victorian visitors with its traditional Turkish-style facilities, colourful mosaic interiors and specialist instruments for spraying the eyes, nose, throat and ears. Today, bathers can enjoy a slightly more appealing facial or chocolate wrap, or relaxing massage in the recently refurbished historic treatment rooms.

494

Enjoy an evening at the fabulous Wilton's Music Hall, which opened its doors in London's East End in 1858, and is the worlds oldest survivng music hall. Despite fighting off the effects of old age

Opposite page Left: A Penfold letterbox. Top right: The interior of Harrogate's Royal Baths. Bottom right: Wilton's Music Hall, an authentic night out! This page Top: Go out in style with a 19th-century funeral. Bottom: A Victorian snakes and ladders set.

t continues to delight with its unique atmosphere and a diverse events programme. Theatre, music, comedy, cabaret, film nights and a bar attract a hip London crowd.

495

Down a pint (or a g&t) in one of the country's surviving Victorian gin palaces. The Philharmonic Dining Rooms in Liverpool retains much of its grand 1898 panelled and copper-trimmed interior. The men's lavatories boast impressive marble urinals which can be viewed by guided tour.

496

Experience the Victorian education system at the British Schools Museum in Hitchin. Philanthropist William Wilshere opened the school in 1810 to help educate children of the working poor. Today, visitors can write on a slate, dip an old-fashioned pen in an ink well and play Victorian games.

497

Ride side saddle. Fancy making a theatrical entrance? This unusual but romantic method of transport continues to attract enthusiasts, plus a riding habit is *so* flattering. Both the Liberty Side Saddle Network and the Side Saddle Association are dedicated to the cause. Although it's said to be easier than riding astride, lessons before trying at home are highly recommended!

498

Immerse yourself in the era at Blists Hill Victorian Town, Ironbridge Gorge, Shropshire. Change your money into old-style coins for the day and spend happily as you wander Victorian streets, meeting Victorian-clad townsfolk and shop-keepers, play in the 19th-century traditional funfair, drink in a Victorian pub, and ride in a horse and cart, before going home with a nice sticky bag of liquorice, gob stoppers and pear drops from the Victorian sweetshop.

499

Play Snakes and Ladders This board game from India, designed to teach players about the Hindu religion, was published in the United Kingdom in the 1890s. It retained a moral tone: players on squares representing virtues such as Penitence and Thrift moved up ladders to Grace and Fulfilment. Landing on the vices, including Indulgence and Disobedience led (via snakes) to Poverty and Disgrace.

500

Make a dramatic exit with your very own Victorian-style funeral. Established in 1881, T Cribb & Sons of East London still offers an authentic 19th- century style funeral service, complete with black-plumed horses and restored Victorian hearses and mourners' carriages.

Index

note: 'V' used as abbreviation for Victoria

Credits

Abbreviations:
b = bottom, c = centre, l = left, r = right, t = top

Front Cover (cropped): The Royal Collection © 2011, Her Majesty Queen Elizabeth II
Back Cover (cropped): © Getty Images/Hulton Archive
Inside front cover (Main picture and inset): © Museum of London
Inside back cover: © Museum of London

Alamy: 136t (©A.F. Archive); 52t (©Pictorial Press); Atelier Works: 138; Bridgeman Art Library: 86l (© Birmingham Museums and Art Gallery; 61 (© Bradford Art Galleries and Museums, UK); 79r (© British Library, London); 106 (© Culture and Sport Glasgow/ Museums); 131r (Deutsches Historiches Museum, Berlin/© DHM Indra Desnica); 141b (Ferens Art Gallery, Hull Museums, UK); 119c (Fitzwilliam Museum, Cambridge, University of Cambridge); 117 (Guildhall Library, City of London); 87b (© Leeds Museums and Galleries, UK); 101tc (© Marylebone Cricket Club, London); 132l (Musée de la Ville de Paris, Musée Carnavalet, Paris/Archives Charmet); 102t (© Museum of London); 68-69, 69bl, 69r, 69tl (National Army Museum, London); 116, 131l (© Private Collection/The Stapleton Collection); 58t, 130l (Private Collection); 120l (Private Collection/© Chris Beetles, London); 59r (Private Collection/ photo © Christie's Images Ltd); 16t (Private Collection/photo © Philip Mould Ltd, London); 44l (Private Collection/photo © Rafael Valls Gallery, London); 87t (Private Collection/The Stapleton Collection); 101bl (© Royal Holloway and Bedford New College); 98 (© United Distillers and Vintners); 90t (© Walker Gallery, National Museums of Liverpool); © British Library Board: 78t, 82r, 120c, 121; © Christie's Images Ltd: 10r, 25br, 65r; © City of London: 60; Corbis Images/ © Bettmann Archive: 130r, 132-3; © Cunard Line: 142br; By Permission of the Trustees of Dulwich Picture Gallery: 11b; © The Francis Frith Collection: 92br, 92tl, 100b; © Getty Images: 135b (Photo by Mark Kauffman/Time Life Pictures); © Getty Images/Hulton Archive: 5, 26b, 27l, 63b, 103bl; Harrogate Borough Council: 148tr; © Historic Royal Palaces: 24r, 134; Historic Royal Palaces/Prudence Cuming Associates © HM Queen Elizabeth II 2001: 35l; Imperial College London, Department of Civil and Environmental Engineering: 77r; © Land of Lost Content/ Heritage-Images/ Imagestate: 133r; © Lebrecht Authors: 78b, 79l; © Lebrecht Music & Arts: 27r; Mary Evans Picture Library:13l, 24tc, 26t, 50, 58b, 59l, 89 (© Interfoto/ Sammlung Rauch), 91 (The Women's Library), 93b, 93t, 94tl, 94tr, 95t, 101tl, 107l, 115t, 118, 120r, 124, 130c, 132c, 147l (National Archives); Mary Evans Picture Library/ILN: 43l, 52bl (© Charlotte Zeepvat), 45r, 53b, 53t, 88r: © Michael Slaughter LRPS: 145b; © Museum of London: 40-41, 47bl, 62-3, 83, 105r; © Museum of London and the Heath family: 100; © National Archives: 107r, 108, 140l; © The National Gallery 2011: 97; © National Portrait Gallery, London: 64br, 64t, 66tr; © Punch Library: 145t; © Robert Opie Collection: 146c, 146r, 147c, 149b; Ronald Grant Archive: 136b (20th Century Fox); 137t (Mrs Brown - BBC/Ecosse Films/ Irish Screen), 137b (The Young Victoria - GK Films); © Royal Botanic Gardens Kew: 66l; The Royal Collection © 2011, Her Majesty Queen Elizabeth II: 2, 10l, 11t (photo: Museum of London), 12l, 12r, 13br, 13tr, 14l, 14r, 15br, 15l, 15tr, 16b, 17b, 17t, 20t, 20-21, 21t, 23, 24l, 25l, 28br, 28-29, 29r (photo: Museum of London), 30l, 30r (photo: Museum of London), 31, 32l, 32r, 33l, 33r, 34l, 34r, 35br, 35tr, 40, 42, 43r, 44r, 45l, 46b, 46t, 47r, 48-49, 48b, 48c, 48tl, 49b, 49t, (photo: Historic Royal Palaces/Robin Forster) 52br, 54, 55l, 55r, 57, 96, 126, 129, 127bl, 127r, 127tl, 128bl, 128br, 128tl; © Royal Geographical Society 2005: 143t; © Royal Horticultural Society/ Lindley Library: 142l, 142tr; Science and Society Picture Library: 67b (© Science Museum); 111 (©NRM Pictorial Collection); 114b (© UIG History); 74r (© National Railway Museum); 114t (© NMR Pictorial Collection); 47tl, 94b (© Science Museum); 115b (© Science Museum Pictorial); © ss Great Britain: 74-5; © Tate, London 2011: 99; T. Cribb & Sons: 149t; © TopFoto: 64bl, 65l, 74l, 84b, 109, 112t, 113b, 113tr, 122t, 135c, 143 (inset); TopFoto/ © AA World Travel: 148l; TopFoto/ © Ann Ronan Picture Library/HIP: 75, 103br; TopFoto/ © British Library/HIP: 73; TopFoto/ © English Heritage/HIP: 110tr; TopFoto/ © Mander and Mitcheson University of Bristol/ArenaPAL: 85r; TopFoto/ © Museum of London/HIP: 80b, 102b; TopFoto/ © National Archives: 105l; TopFoto/ © National Archives/HIP: 71, 80t, 81l, 95b 103tl, 140r; TopFoto/ © Oxford Science Archive: 103tr; TopFoto/ © Roger-Viollet: 84t, 113tl; TopFoto/ © The Granger Collection: 66br, 70-1, 82l, 86r, 86-7, 122b, 123, 141t; TopFoto/ © The Print Collector/HIP: 76l, 101tr, 104t, 104b; TopFoto/ © Ullstein Bild: 76-7; TopFoto/ © United Artists: 135t; TopFoto/ © World History Archive: 67t, 81r, 88l; © V&A Images: 28tl, 40tl, 85l, 90b, 92tr, 110b, 110tl, 112b, 119l, 119r, 144, 146l, 147r; Wilton's Music Hall: 148br;

Published by
Historic Royal Palaces
Hampton Court Palace
Surrey
KT8 9AU

ISBN 978-1-873993-27-9

Edited by
Sarah Kilby
Picture research by
Susan Mennell
Special thanks to
Annie Heron
and **Clare Murphy**
Designed by
Atelier Works
Printed by
BKT

Historic Royal
PALACES

Historic Royal Palaces is the independent charity that looks after the Tower of London, Hampton Court Palace, the Banqueting House, Kensington Palace and Kew Palace. We help everyone explore the story of how monarchs and people have shaped society, in some of the greatest palaces ever built.

We receive no funding from the Government or the Crown, so we depend on the support of our visitors, members, donors, volunteers and sponsors.

Historic Royal Palaces is a registered charity (no. 1068852)

www.hrp.org.uk

Front and back inside covers: sections of the original Descriptive Map of London Poverty, 1889, compiled and hand- coloured by Charles Booth and assistants. Front inside cover shows the varying wealth of streets in Marylebone, Soho, St Giles and Bloomsbury. Back inside cover shows a starkly different picture in Bethnal Green and Whitechapel.